W9-AKA-935

HISTORY OF THE WORLD
Civilizations
of Asia

RAINTREE
STECK-VAUGHN
LIBRARY
A Division of Steck-Vaughn Company

First Steck-Vaughn Edition 1992

This book has been reviewed for accuracy by
Prof. Frank N. Egerton, Dept. of History,
University of Wisconsin-Parkside, Kenosha, Wisconsin.

Published in the United States by Steck-Vaughn Company.

Translated by Hess-Inglin Translation Service.

2 3 4 5 6 7 8 9 93 92 91 90

Library of Congress Number: 88-26385

Printed and bound in the United States of America.

Library of Congress Cataloging-in-Publication Data

Grandi civiltà dell'Asia. English.
Civilizations of Asia.

(History of the World)
Translation of: Le Grandi civiltà dell'Asia.
Includes index.
Summary: Discusses the civilizations of China, Japan, India, Indochina, Indonesia, Australia, and Oceania from the beginnings of time until about A.D. 600.
1. Asia—History—Juvenile literature. 2. Australia—History—Juvenile literature. 3. Oceania—History—Juvenile literature. [1. Asia—History. 2. Australia—History. 3. Oceania—History.] I. Raintree Publishers. II. Title. III. Series.
DS33.5.G7313 1988 950—dc19 88-26385
ISBN 0-8172-3302-4

Cover illustration by Francis Balistreri.

TABLE OF CONTENTS

Years B.C. and A.D.

6000
3500
3000
2500
2300
2000
1700
1500
1100
1000
700
500
400
350
300
250
200
100
50
0
100
200
300
400
500
600

INDIA

PALEOLITHIC
300,000 The most ancient finds

3500 **NEOLITHIC**
From the Iranian plateau, it spreads into India

2300 **CIVILIZATION OF THE INDUS VALLEY**

1700-1500 **ARYAN INVASION**

1000 **VEDIC CIVILIZATION**
First villages and societies
Hinduism

560-486 **BUDDHA and Buddhism**

540-486 Mahavira and Jainism

321 **THE MAYURA EMPIRE**
Founded by Chandragupta

269 Ashoka spreads Buddhism

50 **THE SATAVAHANA EMPIRE**
(Southern India)

50 **THE KUSHAN EMPIRE**
(Northern India) Greek-Indian art
The birth of Hinduism

320 **THE GUPTAN EMPIRE**
Classic age of India

467 The Guptan Empire falls under pressure from the nomads of the steppes

CHINA

PALEOLITHIC
1,800,000 The most ancient finds

6000 **NEOLITHIC**
First agricultural practices
First ceramics

1500 **SHANG DYNASTY**
Bronze artifacts and first towns
Writing

1100 **REIGN OF THE ZHOU**

770 **SPRING AND AUTUMN PERIOD**
Religion

485 **THE WARRING STATES PERIOD**
Confucius, Daoism, and the great lines of thought

221 **QIN, THE FIRST EMPIRE**

206 **THE HAN DYNASTY**
Confucianism societies
The spread of Buddhism
Trade in the Mediterranean
Early classic age in China

220-265 **THE THREE KINGDOMS**
Political division
The importance of the south increases nomadic kingdoms to the north
Increase in Asian trade
Revival of Daoism
The spread of Buddhism

JAPAN

PALEOLITHIC
400,000 The most ancient finds

7000 **EARLY JOMON PERIOD**

1500 **MIDDLE JOMON PERIOD**
Elements of transition toward the Neolithic period

1000 **NEOLITHIC-LATE JOMON**
Rice growing begins

300 **YAYOI EPOCH**
Agriculture blossoms and bronze comes into use

Shinto

300 **AGE OF THE ANCIENT TOMBS**
Widespread use of iron
Wealth and power
Transformation of the society

538-552 Spread of Buddhism

574-622 **THE SHOTOKU REGENCY**
Modernizing the country
The Seventeen Article Constitution
Relationship with China

Asia from the Paleolithic Period to A.D. 600

In blue: late Paleolithic period
In purple-blue: Neolithic period
The colored stripes indicate the influence of the corresponding civilizations.

Indochina

PALEOLITHIC
400,000 The most ancient finds

3000 **NEOLITHIC**
Arrival of populations from China
Rice growing begins

1000 **THE DONG SON CIVILIZATION**
The spread of bronze

Contacts with Indonesia and the Pacific islands begin

300 **INFLUENCE OF INDIA AND CHINA**
Writing, kingdoms, Hinduism and Buddhism, art

center and west

The Indian merchants control the market

250 **THE FUNAN EMPIRE**
Based on commercial and maritime relationships

600 **THE KINGDOM OF TCHENLA**
Early Cambodian Khmer reign

east

250 **EARLY VIETNAMESE KINGDOM**

111 Annexation to China and political-cultural dependence for almost one thousand years

Indonesia

PALEOLITHIC
1,800,000 The most ancient finds

2500 **NEOLITHIC**
Arrival of farming populations from Indochina

500 The spread of bronze from Indochina

250 Influence of the Funan Empire in the north

Australia and Oceania

PALEOLITHIC
30,000 The earliest evidence of settlement in Australia

2000 The settlement of Micronesia and of part of Melanesia

1000 The settlement of all of Melanesia

300 Populating the Marquesas Islands

400 Populating the Hawaiian Islands

800-850 The last islands to be populated

Years B.C. and A.D.

6000
3500
3000
2500
2300
2000
1700
1500
1100
1000
700
500
400
350
300
250
200
100
50
0
100
200
300
400
500
600

ASIA

The Regions of Asia

Asia is made up of the world's largest continent and its many associated islands. It extends from Africa and Europe in the west to the Pacific Ocean in the east and has a variety of climates and landscapes. Mountain chains cross the continent lengthwise, dividing it into several large regions. These include India, China, Indochina, and the steppes of Central Asia. The island portion includes Japan and Indonesia.

Isolated from the ocean, Central Asia has limited rainfall. The northern part is covered by steppes and has enough plant life to feed wandering livestock. The drier southern part is covered by deserts and mountain chains.

India, located south of the Himalayas, is almost a continent in itself. North to south, it stretches for nearly 2,000 miles (3,200 kilometers). Its climate ranges from alpine around the Himalayas to tropical at the coast.

China is found between the ocean and the rest of the Asian landmass. Because of its location, the country's climate is varied. Seasonal temperatures, for example, are greatly different. Winters in China are much colder than any place in India. Rainfall is also varied. In the north, farming is done on dry land. To the south, in the Yangtze basin and the surrounding mountains, water is abundant.

Indochina is crossed by forest-covered mountain chains running parallel to the coast. Here, human settlements are scarce, except for a few wide inland plateaus, coastal plains, and river deltas. To the east stretch a series of islands separated by channels and internal seas.

The Monsoons

Monsoons are the main influence on the climate of India and all the far eastern regions, from the equator to the temperate areas of the north, where the effects of the ocean climate are more important. From October to May, it rains very little in India. The land becomes dry, the temperature rises, and a hot wind blows. In June, the rain begins and falls for longer than two months. The temperature drops, and the plant life is revived. All over the far east, the monsoons carry humid ocean air northward in the summer, causing the rain and the hot climate.

Australia

Beyond Indonesia is Australia. This island is a relatively young land. Humans settled there only recently.

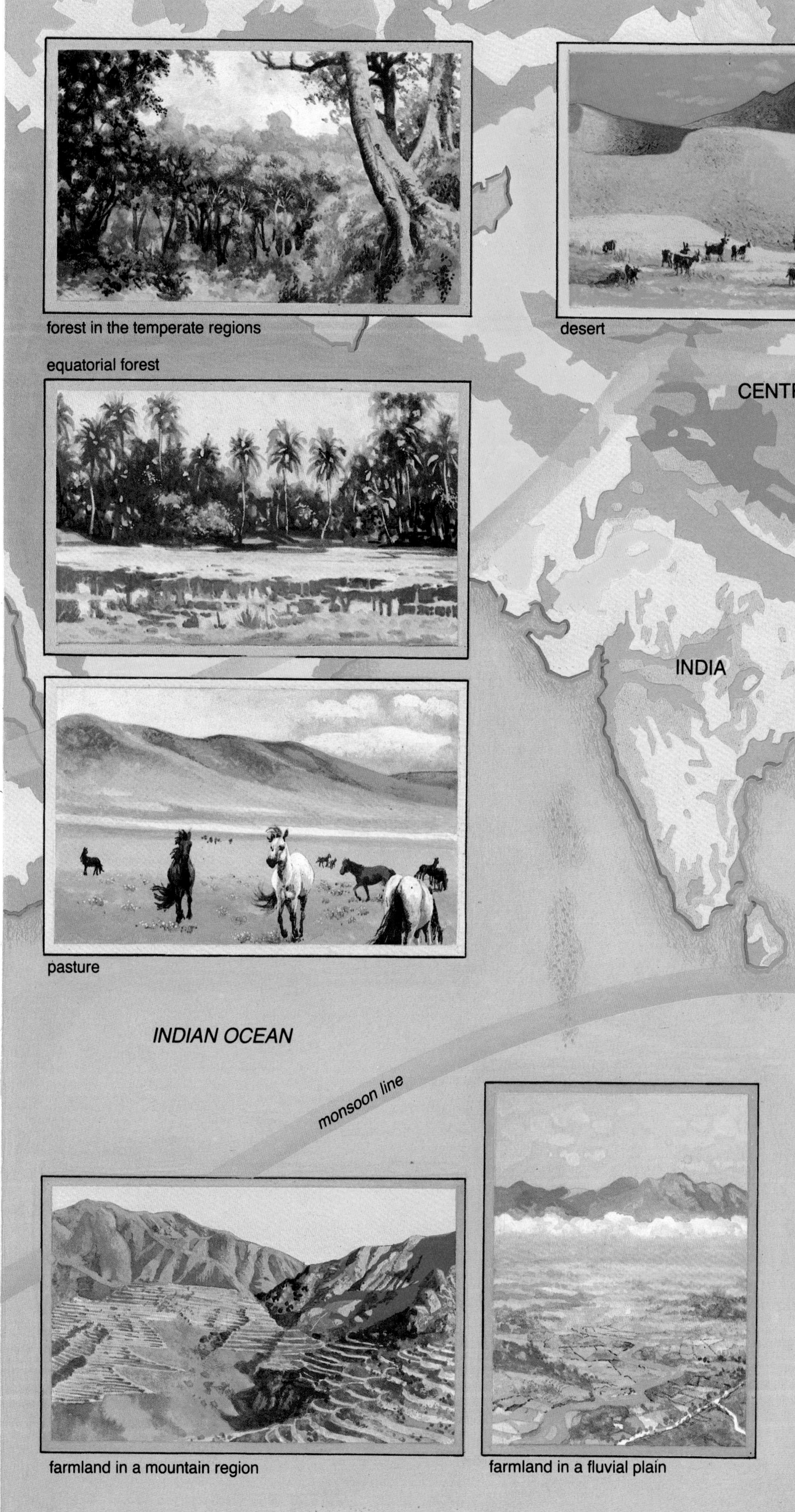

forest in the temperate regions

desert

equatorial forest

pasture

farmland in a mountain region

farmland in a fluvial plain

JAPAN
monsoon line
PACIFIC OCEAN
monsoon line
volcano
CHINA
ASIA
PHILIPPINES
INDOCHINA
steppe of central Asia
INDONESIA
Indian savanna
monsoon line
farmland
pasture
desert
AUSTRALIA
woods, equatorial forest, savannas
barren high mountain areas
steppe
volcanoes and volcanic areas
monsoon zone enclosed
within the shaded lines
high mountains

THE PALEOLITHIC PERIOD

Asia, The Ancient Land of Humanity

Asia was once thought by some to be the cradle of humanity. In 1891 in Java, Eugéne Dubois, a Dutch army surgeon, discovered the remains of a prehistoric human being. Experts considered this creature, called Java man, to be one of the links between humans and monkeys. Years later, however, similar remains over two million years old were found in Africa. From research done at sites there, the stages of human evolution can now be identified. First came *Homo habilis,* a savanna hunter who lived in groups and built simple dwellings. Then came *Homo erectus,* who discovered fire, perfected stone tools, and formed more complicated thoughts and ideas. Finally, *Homo sapiens* developed.

Homo Erectus in Java and China

So far, no fossil remains of *Homo habilis* have been found in Asia. The most ancient fossil find in Java is 1,800,000 years old. It is called Meganthroupus, but experts are not sure whether it is an ancestor of *Homo erectus* or if it belongs to an earlier group of creatures known as australopithecines. The most ancient groups of *Homo erectus* were present in Java about 1,100,000 years ago.

Northern China is another important source of *Homo erectus* remains and has even provided evidence of the stone tools that were used. Two teeth found in the Yunnan province date back 1,700,000 years. Lantian man, discovered in Shaanxi, appeared about 700,000 years ago. The famous Peking man, or Sinanthropus, found in 1921 in Zhoukoudian, lived more recently than the others. This group lived between 500,000 and 200,000 years ago and left behind the remains of over forty individuals.

Homo Sapiens in China

As *Homo sapiens* evolved, groups of these people spread all over China. They had highly perfected tools, especially by the end of the Paleolithic period and in the Mesolithic period. All over northern China, finely crafted blades, called microliths, were made. They were mounted on bone or wooden handles and were precise, useful tools. Evidence of fireplaces used during this period has been discovered, as well as the remains of seasonal hunters' camps.

The Paleolithic Period in India and Japan

No fossil remains prior to the Mesolithic period have been found in India. What scientists know about the country's ancient human settlements comes from the many stone tools found there. The oldest of these tools, found in the Soan River area, are large, slightly sharpened pebbles from 200,000 to 300,000 years ago. Later, especially in the southern regions, tools grew more advanced. These tools, called bifacial tools, were sharpened on both sides.

The oldest Japanese stone tools, which are about 400,000 years old, are pebbles with sharp, rough-cut edges. These were found in the prefecture of Oita. Pebbles of this kind are found in successive soil layers.

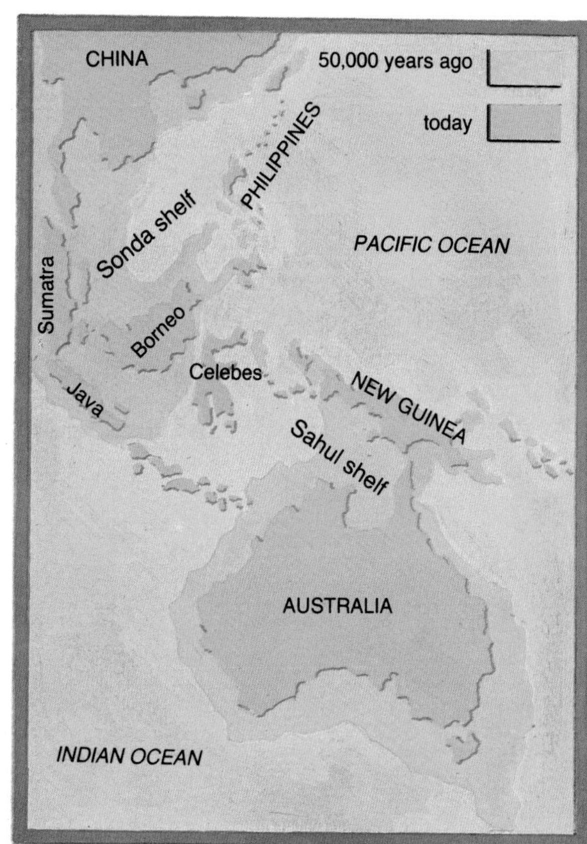

This map shows the lands above sea level in southeast Asia and Australia.

Populating Southeast Asia and Australia

The remains of *Homo erectus* in Indochina are more than 400,000 years old. Between 30,000 and 10,000 B.C., *Homo sapiens* appeared in the Philippines, Borneo, and Java. Here, by 20,000 B.C., the so-called Wadjak man had features similar to those of the Australian populations living today. Within about thirty thousand years of the end of the Paleolithic period, humans populated Australia.

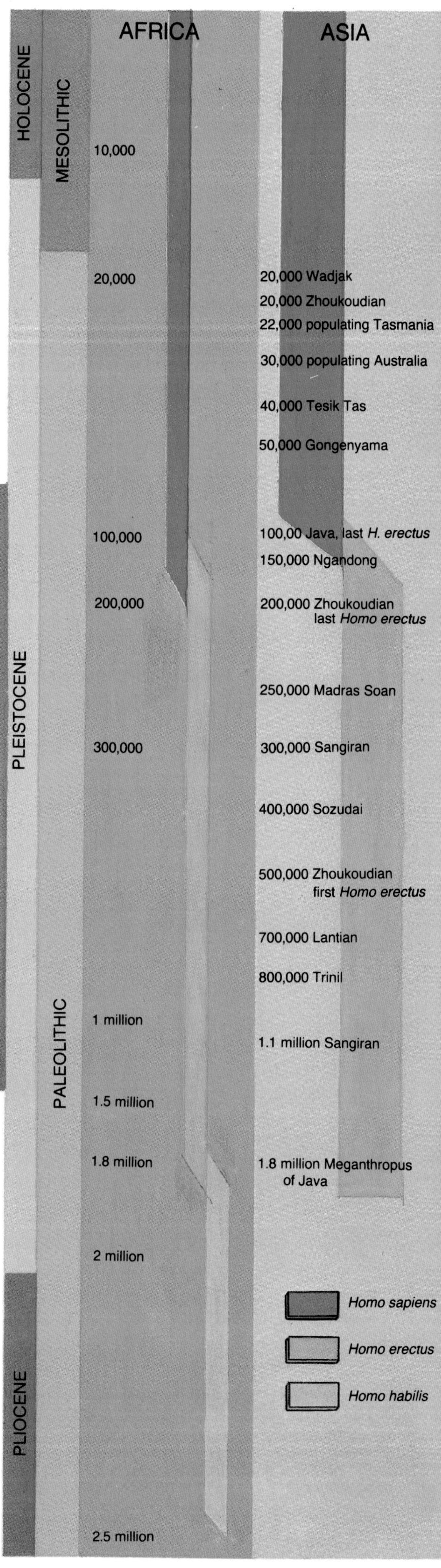

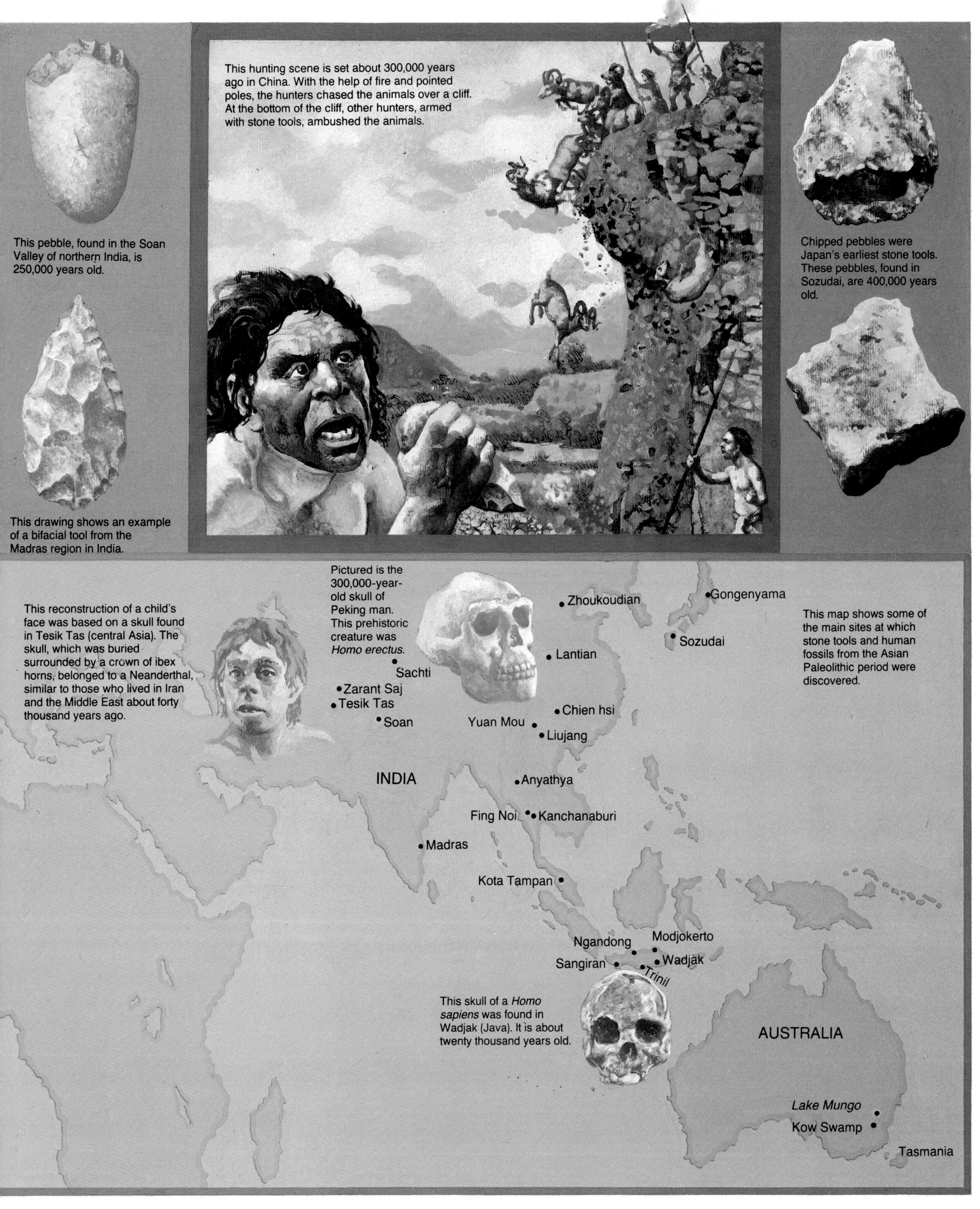

This pebble, found in the Soan Valley of northern India, is 250,000 years old.

This drawing shows an example of a bifacial tool from the Madras region in India.

This hunting scene is set about 300,000 years ago in China. With the help of fire and pointed poles, the hunters chased the animals over a cliff. At the bottom of the cliff, other hunters, armed with stone tools, ambushed the animals.

Chipped pebbles were Japan's earliest stone tools. These pebbles, found in Sozudai, are 400,000 years old.

This reconstruction of a child's face was based on a skull found in Tesik Tas (central Asia). The skull, which was buried surrounded by a crown of ibex horns, belonged to a Neanderthal, similar to those who lived in Iran and the Middle East about forty thousand years ago.

Pictured is the 300,000-year-old skull of Peking man. This prehistoric creature was *Homo erectus.*

This map shows some of the main sites at which stone tools and human fossils from the Asian Paleolithic period were discovered.

This skull of a *Homo sapiens* was found in Wadjak (Java). It is about twenty thousand years old.

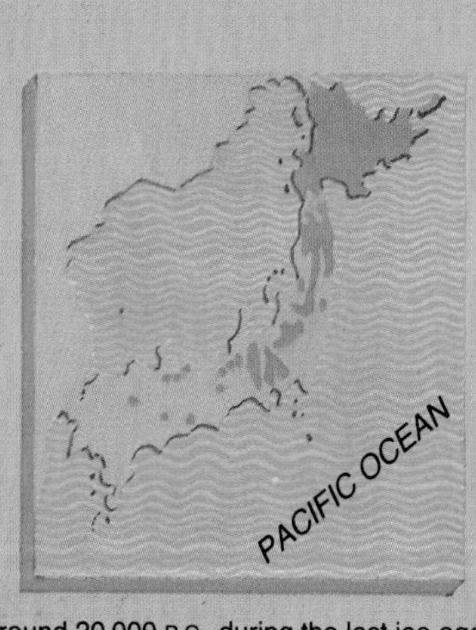

Around 20,000 B.C., during the last ice age, Japan was still connected to the continent. The glaciers are shown in green.

By 10,000 B.C., Japan has completely separated from the continent but still has a close relationship with it. Influences from the continent come through the ancient land routes. To the north, Japan is influenced by Siberia; to the south, by China and Korea.

In this illustration, a hunter skins a moose in southern Japan about twenty thousand years ago. In the background, smoke rises from an active volcano.

The legend bar *(above)* shows the major periods of prehistory in Japan.

The giant deer and the mammoth were typical animals in prehistoric Japan. During the glaciations, they migrated to Japan. The deer came from Korea; the mammoth came from the northern lands.

JAPAN FROM THE PALEOLITHIC PERIOD TO THE MIDDLE JOMON PERIOD

The Birth of the Archipelago of Japan

Japan, as it is known today, is an archipelago formed by four major islands and numerous smaller islands. This arrangement emerged very recently.

In ancient times, Japan was part of the Euro-Asiatic continent. From the Kamchatka Peninsula to Indonesia, the land facing the Pacific Ocean stretched in a continuous line. But little by little, the gradual rise of the wide China plain caused rift valleys to appear. These rifts filled with ocean water. In this way, the Okhotsk Sea, the Japan Sea, and the China Sea were formed, separating the coast from the inner land. Japan was already displaying a "sickle" shape 500,000 years ago and by then was connected to the continent only by its northern and southern tips. In the meantime, the land kept changing: the Pacific rifts grew deeper, small pieces of land separated from the continent, and the territory of Japan, shaken by violent volcanic activity, broke into many islands. Japan probably became totally isolated around fifteen thousand years ago.

Evolution of the Paleolithic Age in Japan

It was once thought that people appeared in Japan only recently. But fossils and stones found in the past few decades are evidence of much earlier human settlements. Today, sites dating back to the Paleolithic period have been discovered throughout Japan.

Fossil remains of Japan's early inhabitants show some Neanderthal features. These Paleolithic people spread throughout Japan while the land was still changing. They most certainly saw

Three vases of the middle Jomon (1500-1000 B.C.) display rope decorations typical of this period.

7000 PROTO JOMON | 5000 EARLY JOMON | 1500 MIDDLE JOMON | 1000 RECENT AND LATE JOMON | 500 B.C.

By the seaside, men and women of the early Jomon period gather shells. In the foreground is a heap of empty shells. Huge piles of these discarded shells have been found throughout Japan. To the right stand the huts of a primitive village. These huts were built partially underground and had roofs of hay.

some amazing natural occurrences. In the Gumma region, cut stones typical of the late Paleolithic period were found in ash layers, in hardened lava flows, or under major eruptions.

Evolution of the Mesolithic Period

During this period, hunting was still the main means of survival, but the tools changed greatly. From the simple pebbles of the late Paleolithic period came the finely crafted tools of the Mesolithic period, which started around 13,000 B.C. These changes, along with the appearance of new objects, suggest that trading routes—either by land or by river—also began at this time.

The Early and Middle Jomon Period

As people's skills and the trade routes developed, a new way of life began in Japan. This new period was known for its simple pottery and the method of decorating it, which called for using ropes. In fact, this method gave the Jomon period its name. In Japanese, *Jomon* means "rope decoration."

As the Jomon period began (around 7000 B.C.), the human population continued to expand. People began to settle for long periods in places where their needs could be met. A typical settlement was found at the foot of a hill, close to a river, or on the seashore. There, the mountains offered caves or other shelters. The forest-covered slopes were filled with game. The river and the sea supplied fish and shellfish, which were a main part of the human diet.

In spite of cold winters and hot summers, Japan's natural wealth made life easy. Because of this, it was many years before people learned to depend on farming for their food. Until the middle Jomon period (around 1000 B.C.), the people were too well fed with fish to worry about starting a farming economy. Nevertheless, villages started to appear. These were groups of huts, partially underground, with roofs made of plant matter.

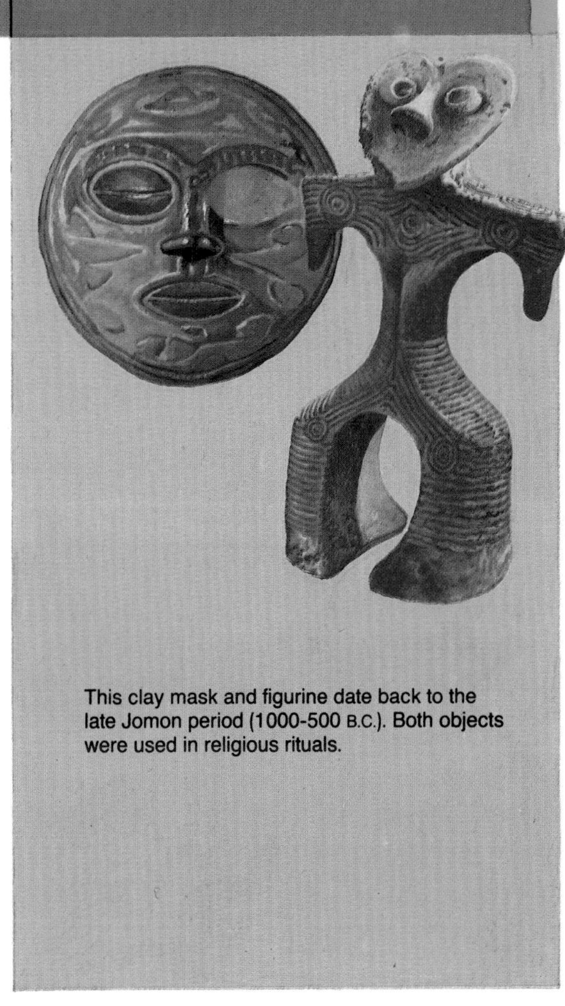

This clay mask and figurine date back to the late Jomon period (1000-500 B.C.). Both objects were used in religious rituals.

Beginning around 1600 B.C., rice was grown in the moist areas of the Yangtze River basin.

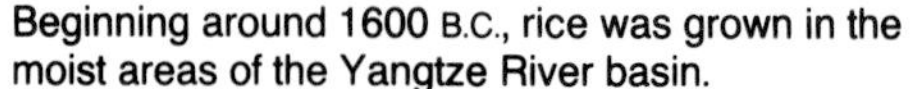

This Neolithic village in northern China is surrounded by a ditch used for protection from wild animals.

THE NEOLITHIC PERIOD IN CHINA

The Birth of Agriculture and Ceramics

Remains of the early Neolithic societies are clearly visible in the Huang He (Yellow River) basin. There, human communities became closely tied to the land. At first this tie was temporary, but then they abandoned the nomadic life completely. The most ancient cultures in the Huang He basin date back to 6000 B.C.

Typical artifacts of these first communities are simple clay objects decorated with impressions of rope, wicker, or combs. These ceramics are very different from the beautiful vases of the Yangshao culture that eventually developed in the Henan Province. By the time this culture developed, the shapes created and the materials used were much more refined.

At this time, villages started appearing. In northern China, they were numerous and close-set. In fact, excavations show that they were often not more than six miles apart. Some were large, such as Banpo, which stretched 7 acres (3 hectares), or Lintong, which covered 12 acres (5 ha). Some were surrounded by streams or ditches as protection against wild animals or human attackers.

Little by little, the shape of the houses changed from circular to square, and they were eventually built more above ground. Wooden columns or poles supported a thatched roof, and a central hole served as a chimney. As the roofs rose above ground level, the walls were built of a mixture of clay, stones, and hay placed between wooden poles. Finally, many villages also had a community house. This larger, square building was often found at the village's center.

The Growth of the Culture

China's climate, which was once warmer than it is today, favored the development of agricul-

This bone plowshare belonging to the Hemudu culture dates back to 5000 B.C.

These two ritual objects of jade were found in the Yangtze River basin. On the left is a Zong, the use of which is still unknown. Below is an ax from 2500-2000 B.C.

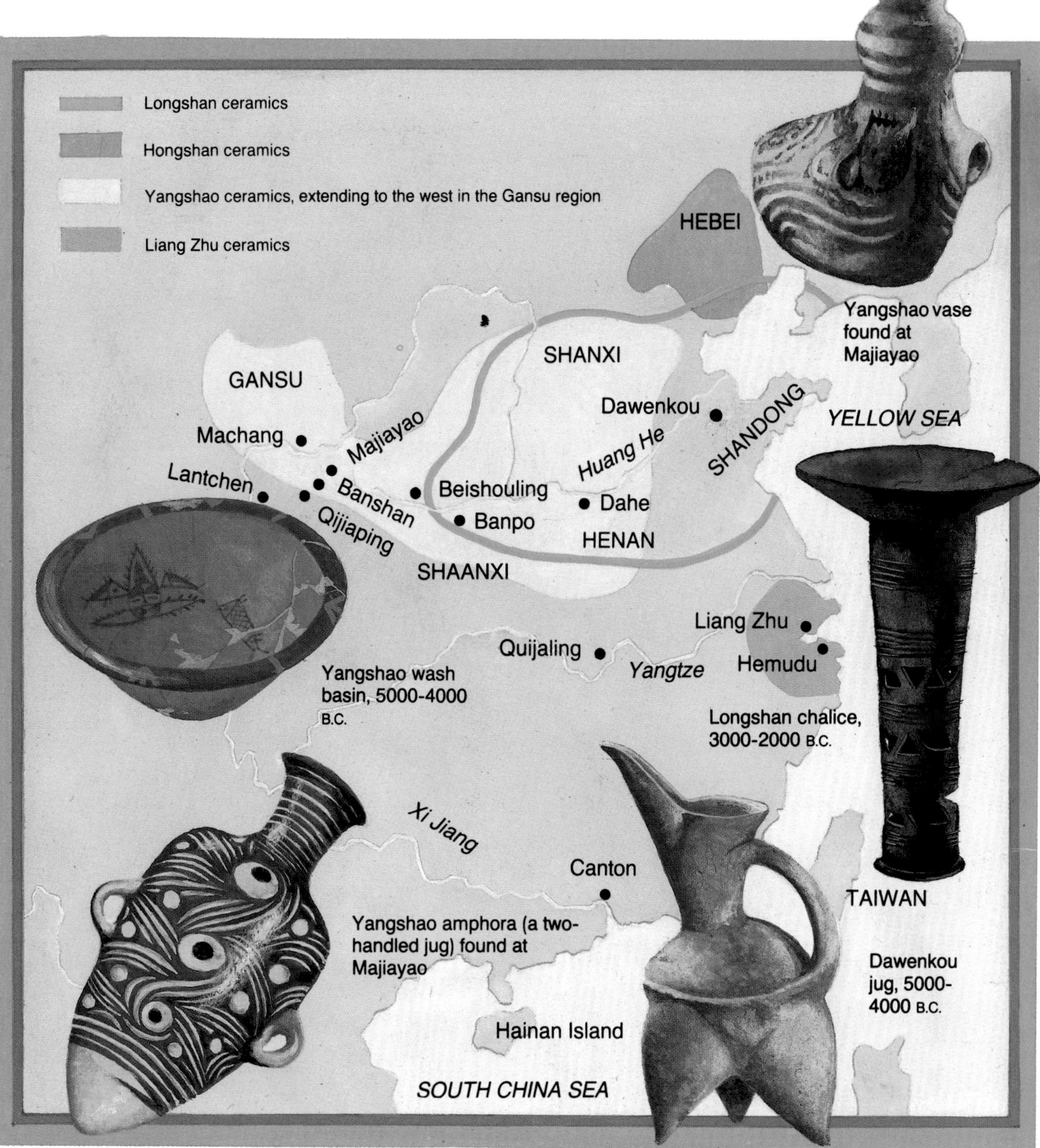

This map shows the most important centers of the Chinese Neolithic period and the areas where different types of ceramics developed and overlapped.

A carved jade bracelet

These stone axes from the middle of the third millennium B.C., were found near Hong Kong in southern China.

This painted ceramic vase was found in the Gansu Province along the course of the Wei River. The decorations are believed to be the most ancient Chinese image of a dragon.

ture. In the middle and lower basin of the Yangtze, rice was grown as early as 5000 B.C. About the same time, around the Huang He, millet was domesticated. The gathering of vegetables, hunting, and fishing completed the diet. A settled life-style and free time in slow farming months helped people develop such crafts as weaving, ceramics, and dyeing.

The Chinese life-style was moving forward at a great rate. At the same time, its past also grew important as people showed an increasing interest in and respect for their ancestors and the dead. Children who died or who were sacrificed in rituals during construction of a home were put in jars and buried inside the house or nearby. Older children and adults were buried in special sites, in tombs, or in large jars. Neolithic cemeteries also show that women played an important role in Chinese society. Often burials of women outnumbered those of men. Through the centuries, however, the number of male burials grew as more importance was given to men in social life.

Changes Around the End of the Neolithic Period

By 2700 B.C., people were skilled in using the potter's wheel. With it, they produced a new kind of ceramic that was thin, shiny, and often only one color. The most beautiful examples of this period come from the sites of Dawenkou and Longshan in the Shandong Province. Also at this time, people domesticated, or tamed, horses and sheep.

It is difficult to trace the progress of the human populations that lived outside the central areas. It is certain, though, that the groups in the various regions were very active, from the Yangshao culture on the upper Huang He to the complex Yangtze cultures (at Daxi and Qujialing) and those of the Canton region. All these groups shared in the flourishing agriculture and crafts. For example, improved kilns and the expert management of fire quickly spread the use of bronze around 1500 B.C. Such activities moved Chinese culture quickly ahead.

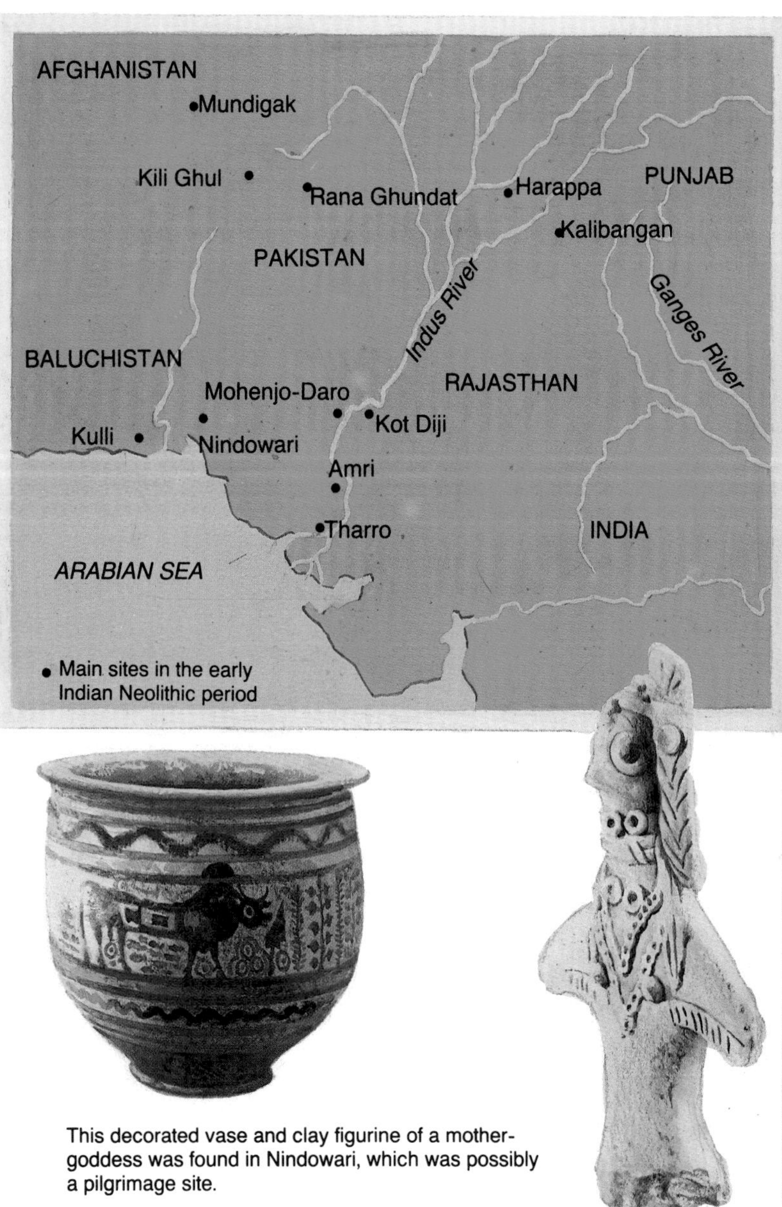

This decorated vase and clay figurine of a mother-goddess was found in Nindowari, which was possibly a pilgrimage site.

The introduction of agriculture changed everyday life as seen in one of northwestern India's first villages.

The Neolithic Period in India and Southeast Asia

A Major Change in India

After the Ice Age, important changes took place all over southern Asia. Around the end of the Paleolithic period and the beginning of the Mesolithic period, people in India specialized in various kinds of fishing and hunting of both large and small animals. Wild plants became an important food source, and grains were gathered to be ground or chopped. The people also designed tools to cut stones, wood, bones, and pelts. The most important of these tools was the microlith, a small, finely cut stone blade made of quartz or flint.

The signs of a major change were in the air. In Rajasthan, domesticated sheep and goats became an important part of the economy. New cooking methods were invented, and from time to time, the first rudimentary forms of hand-modeled pottery appeared. By this time, people lived in huts with walls made of cane and covered with mud. They began to settle permanently and made the first attempts at farming. Trees were felled and burned, and the land was farmed for short periods, with the growing of rice beginning in the Ganges valley.

The Birth of Agriculture

This way of life was to continue for a long time in India, especially in the more remote central and southern regions. To the west of the Iranian plateau, however, agriculture gradually advanced. The most ancient traces of farming and stable settlements east of Iran were found in Afghanistan and Pakistan and date back to 3500-3000 B.C. These farming populations were probably small scattered groups, who brought new methods from Iran. At first, they established nomadic camps, but little by little, villages grew. Houses were first made of clay and later of bricks, and the size of the villages slowly increased. Potters' wheels were used to manufacture vases, and the first copper tools appeared. These people also kept some animals such as goats, hogs, and cows.

Villages spread throughout the Iranian plateau and into Baluchistan. To the north, the populations of farmers were stopped by the mountains, but they were able to settle in the Punjab region. From there, they moved toward the plains, developing more and more devices with which to control water.

All of the human settlements were the size of villages, with the exception of Mundigak, in what is today Afghanistan. Within a few centuries, this network of settlements would grow to become the valley's first cities.

On an inland Indochina plateau, colonists from the north slash part of a forest for farming.

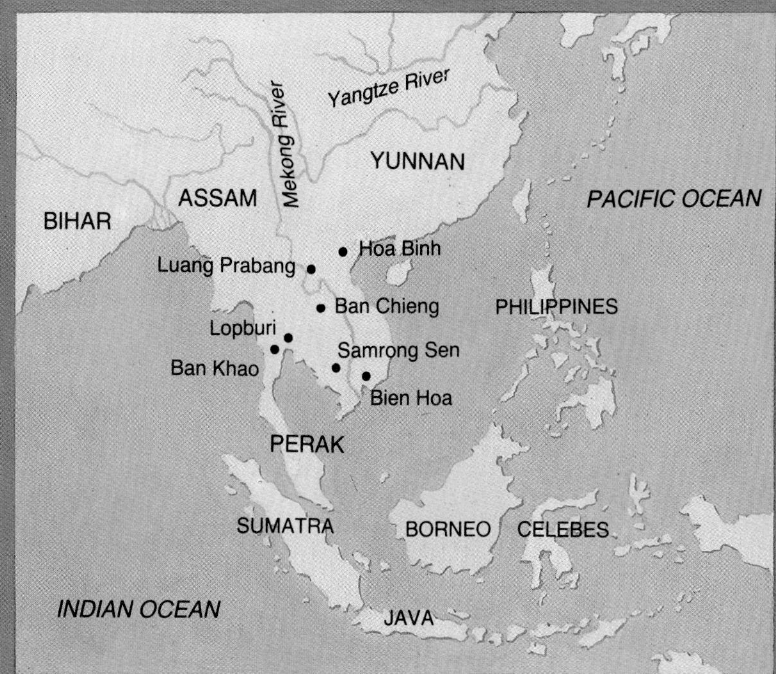

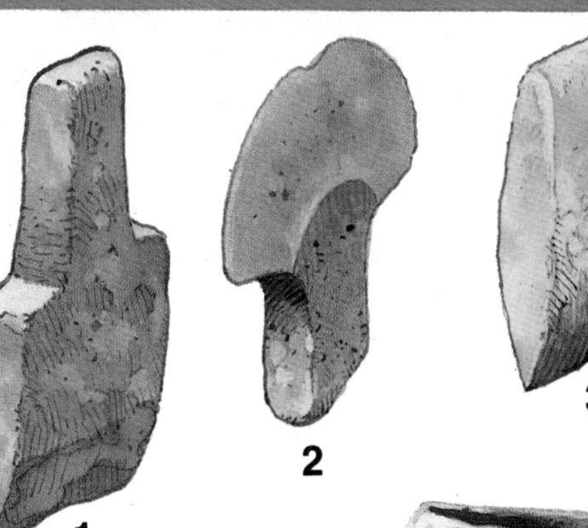

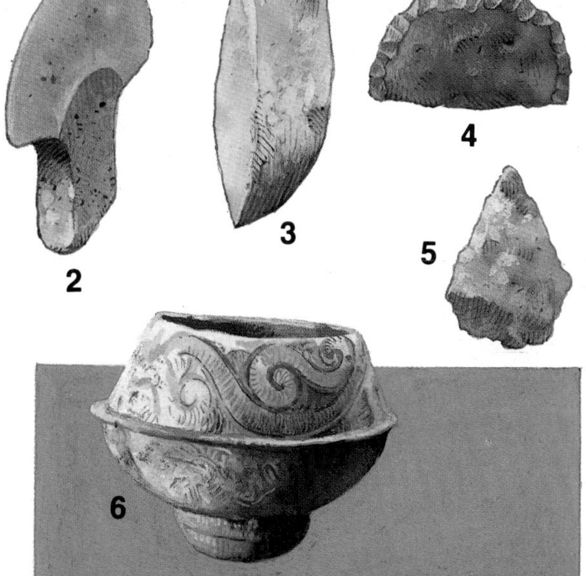

1) shoulder ax from Samrong Sen; 2) stone tool from Luang Prabang; 3) jade bifacial from Yunnan; 4) scraper from Som Jo, near Hoa Binh; 5) arrowhead from Trieng-Xen, near Hoa Binh; 6-7) Neolithic clay bowls from Ban Chieng; 8) Neolithic vase from Ban Chieng.

The Mesolithic Period in Southeast Asia

After the glaciations, the Indochina peninsula became more accessible. Between 5000 and 3000 B.C., people spread throughout this region, bringing with them new ideas and techniques. Their tools were more finely crafted, and the materials used to make them were chosen with more care. These people, who probably came from southern China, later spread toward the Pacific islands. The site of Hoa Binh is especially rich in finds from this group. Almost at the same time, another migrating group of people moved southward. They were using short axes with smoothed blades and other tools made of mother of pearl or bone. They already knew a primitive form of pottery. These people were named after the Bacson region, where numerous burial caves were uncovered. They left traces of their passage throughout the peninsula and even as far away as Indonesia.

The Spread of Agriculture

With agriculture's introduction, people's lifestyles became similar in different populations. For example, rice cultivation started at roughly the same time here as in China and India, perhaps even before. But this was not the extent of this movement's influence. Better farming methods also called for better tools. Axes, which were at first egg shaped, were now shaped like diamonds. Many of these axes also had extensions, which made it easier to tie them to handles. With improved tools, woodworking and ceramics were perfected between 2500 and 1000 B.C. Ceramics, in particular, became widespread.

From the mountain regions, people moved toward the lowlands and the open plains, becoming more and more skilled in farming. They still grew rice on dry land but also learned to control water flow. This allowed rice to be grown on flooded fields, which brought a bigger crop.

This soapstone seal from Harappa was crafted about 3000 B.C. It is decorated with a unicorn and pictographs, a primitive form of writing.

This bronze statuette, found in Mohenjo-Daro, depicts a young dancer.

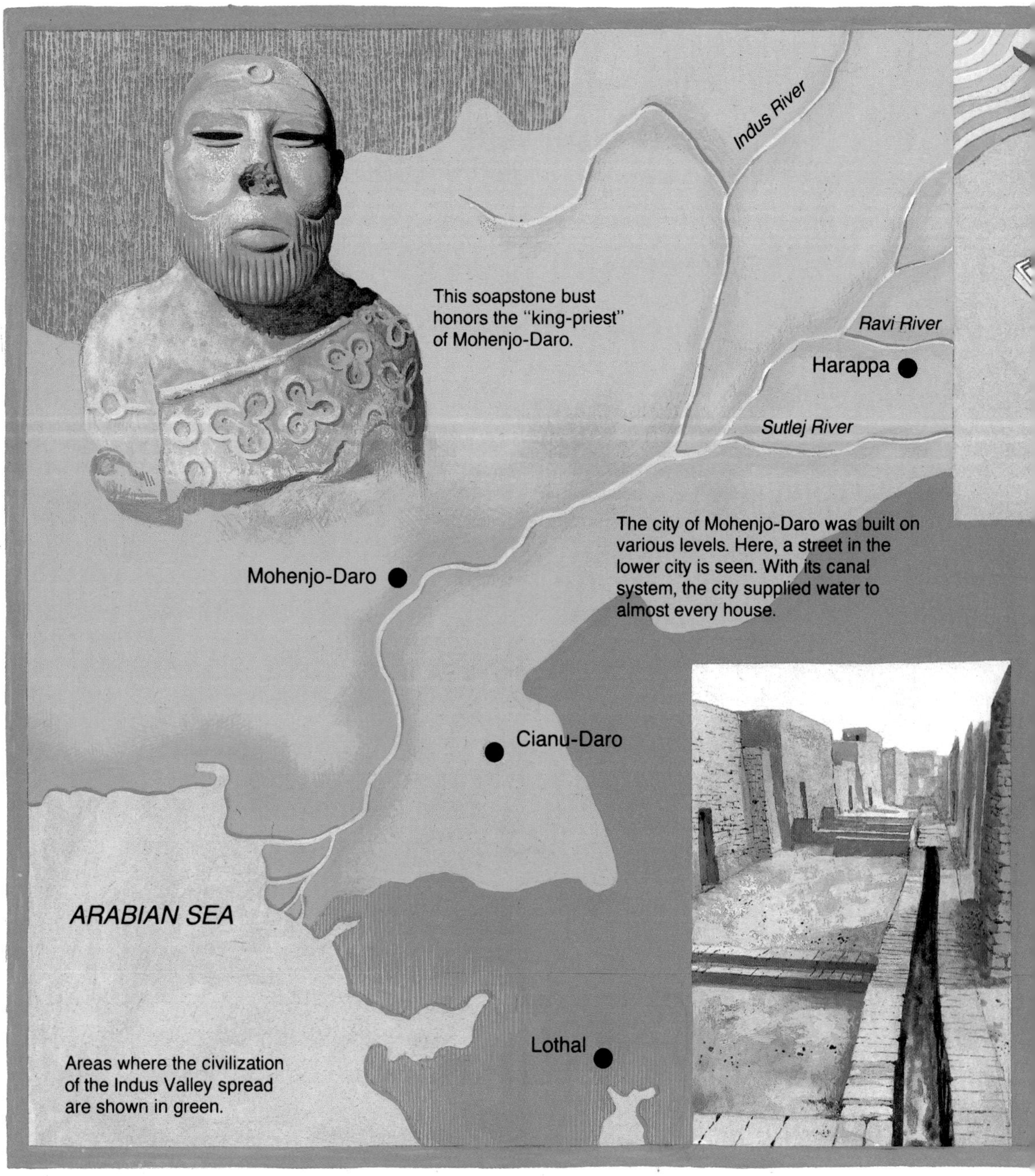

This soapstone bust honors the "king-priest" of Mohenjo-Daro.

Indus River

Ravi River

Harappa

Sutlej River

Mohenjo-Daro

Cianu-Daro

Lothal

ARABIAN SEA

The city of Mohenjo-Daro was built on various levels. Here, a street in the lower city is seen. With its canal system, the city supplied water to almost every house.

Areas where the civilization of the Indus Valley spread are shown in green.

To the left: The peoples of the Indus Valley did not burn their dead on pyres. They buried them underground. This drawing reconstructs a burial chamber found in Harappa.

THE CIVILIZATION OF THE INDUS VALLEY

Urban Civilization Blossoms

Around 2500 B.C., an urban civilization blossomed in the wide area between Pakistan and the Indian states of Punjab and Gujarat. Earlier, this same area had seen farming practices develop and the first villages appear. This urban civilization had complex forms of art and religion, and its cities were equipped with sewers, barns, and sanitary facilities.

The existence of such an advanced civilization in India, which had not yet suffered the Indo-European invasions, was unknown until the first decades of this century. Eventually, through excavations led by the English archaeologist Sir John Marshall, this civilization's remains were uncovered. Though a great amount of material was found in these excavations, not much is yet known about the civilization. For example, the writing of the Indus Valley civilization (so called because its towns were erected along the course of the Indus River) has not yet been deciphered. Experts have tried to break the code working with pictographs found on seals and graffiti. But so far, no final results have been obtained.

As for the ethnic nature of the Indus Valley people, it is likely that they belonged to the Dravida family. This group of humans appeared in India during ancient times. The people had dark complexions and long, straight hair. They were of medium height and spoke a variety of "Dravidan" languages or dialects.

The main centers of this civilization were the cities of Harappa and Mohenjo-Daro. Although over 300 miles (500 km) apart, these two cities showed many similarities in their cultures. These similarities were due to an easy communication along the river routes and a common government under the same political and religious authority. The urban social structure of Harappa and Mohenjo-Daro was based on an economy of trading and agriculture. The main crops were wheat and barley, as shown by barns which were found during excavations in Mohenjo-Daro. As for the military structure, the Indus

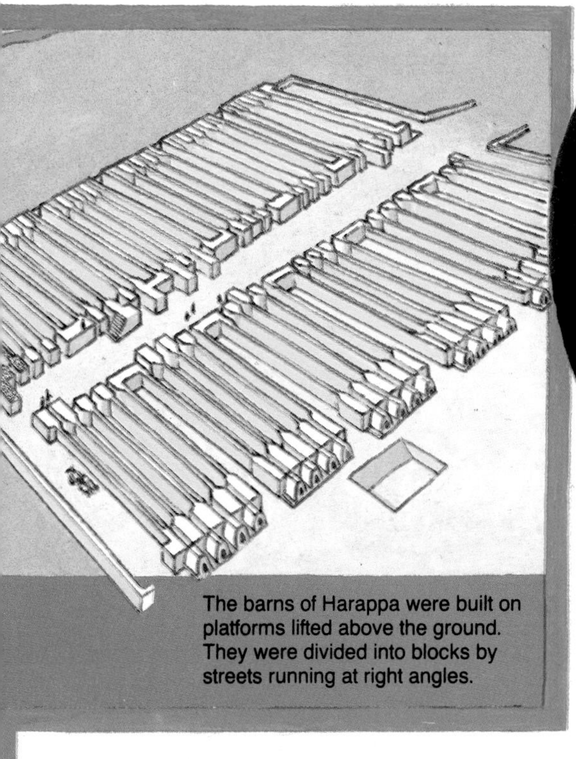

The barns of Harappa were built on platforms lifted above the ground. They were divided into blocks by streets running at right angles.

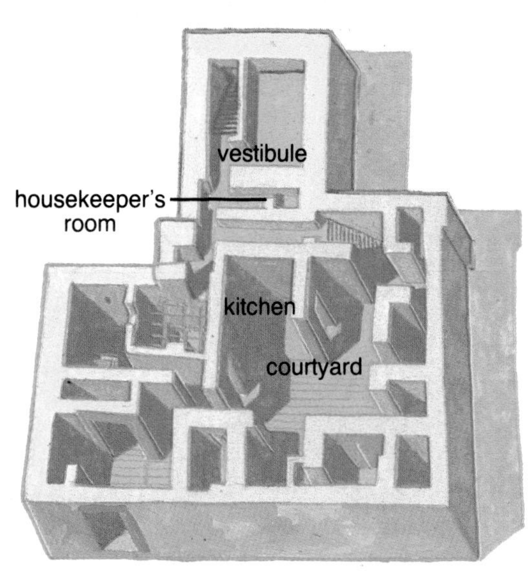

This drawing shows the ground floor of an average house in Mohenjo-Daro. Note the vestibule and the room for the housekeeper. The central courtyard was paved with bricks. Around the courtyard were the small servants' rooms and the kitchen. The master's quarters were on the first floor.

Above: An artist reconstructs the city of Mohenjo-Daro at the height of splendor, around 2000 B.C. A fortress stands in the foreground. The houses here are rather large. In the lower part of the city, the workers lived in crowded quarters. Their houses had only two rooms. *Far above:* This soapstone seal, from Mohenjo-Daro, dates back to the third millennium B.C.

Valley civilization seems to have been completely peaceful. The few weapons found seem more likely to have been used for hunting than for war.

Art and Religion

Experts working on the Indus Valley excavations have noted many surprising similarities between that culture and more recent cultures. Art found in the Indus Valley, for example, closely resembles Indian art of the last 1,500 years. In addition, religious figurines found in Harappa and Mohenjo-Daro are very like those of Hinduism, a later religion. Evidence of cults surrounding a Great Goddess, trees, water, and a male divinity further suggest a connection between this early religion and Hinduism, which has similar cults in its teachings. The fact that Hinduism did not emerge as a religion until hundreds of years after the end of the Indus civilization is a question puzzling many archaeologists.

The End of the Indus Valley Civilization

The Indus Valley civilization, so highly civilized and modern, suddenly disappeared around 1500 B.C. It appears that after a short decline, it quickly collapsed and faded away. Scholars have several ideas to explain the causes of such an event. One possible cause was the arrival of warlike Indo-European tribes. These tribes violently colonized northwestern India. Some scholars suggest that the invaders coming from the plains of the Ganges may have destroyed vital water sources. Still other sources suggest that some sort of ecological disaster due to deforestation caused the civilization's collapse. Perhaps the answer is a combination of all these factors.

Map above: Around 1500 B.C., numerous groups of Indo-European nomadic tribes came from the west. They spread through and conquered the territories of the Indus Valley civilization. Some of them continued on to the plains of the Ganges.

An Indo-European village thrives near a riverbank. The houses are made of clay with roofs of hay. In the foreground, father and son go home in a chariot pulled by oxen. Beyond them, a man is plowing wetland by the river, and some women are doing laundry. On the threshing-floor in front of the houses, rice is bolted and then stored under a shelter. Boats, seen sailing the river, provide one of the main means of transportation for people and goods. Originally nomadic shepherds, the Indo-European tribes eventually settled in India. Here they learned to combine livestock-rearing and agriculture, abandoning nomadism. The villages which developed at that time (1500-1000 B.C.) are still a typical feature of Indian life today.

INDIA: THE INDO-EUROPEAN SOCIETY

The Arrival of the Indo-Europeans

At around 1500 B.C., the Indus Valley civilization disappeared. About this same time, India was invaded by several waves of a nomadic and rather warlike population coming from the west. In general, the invaders' movement was from west to east, with small digressions to the south. The military superiority of these peoples was mainly based on the use of war chariots pulled by one or more horses.

Within a rather short time (1500 to 1000 B.C.), the Indo-European tribes occupied the whole Indus River region, most of the plains through which the Ganges River flows (north-central India), and some neighboring regions. The newcomers, called Aryans, were nomadic tribes living as herders and hunters. Their simple, unrefined culture thus took the place of the highly developed culture of the Indus Valley. But once they reached India, they very quickly settled and built stable villages.

On the Indian continent, more particularly in its north-central regions, these tribes lived in villages with a square layout. Often these villages were well protected and had entrances at the four main points. Their houses were built with wood, bamboo, or clay. These materials were also used for cult and meeting dwellings. Because of the perishable nature of these con-

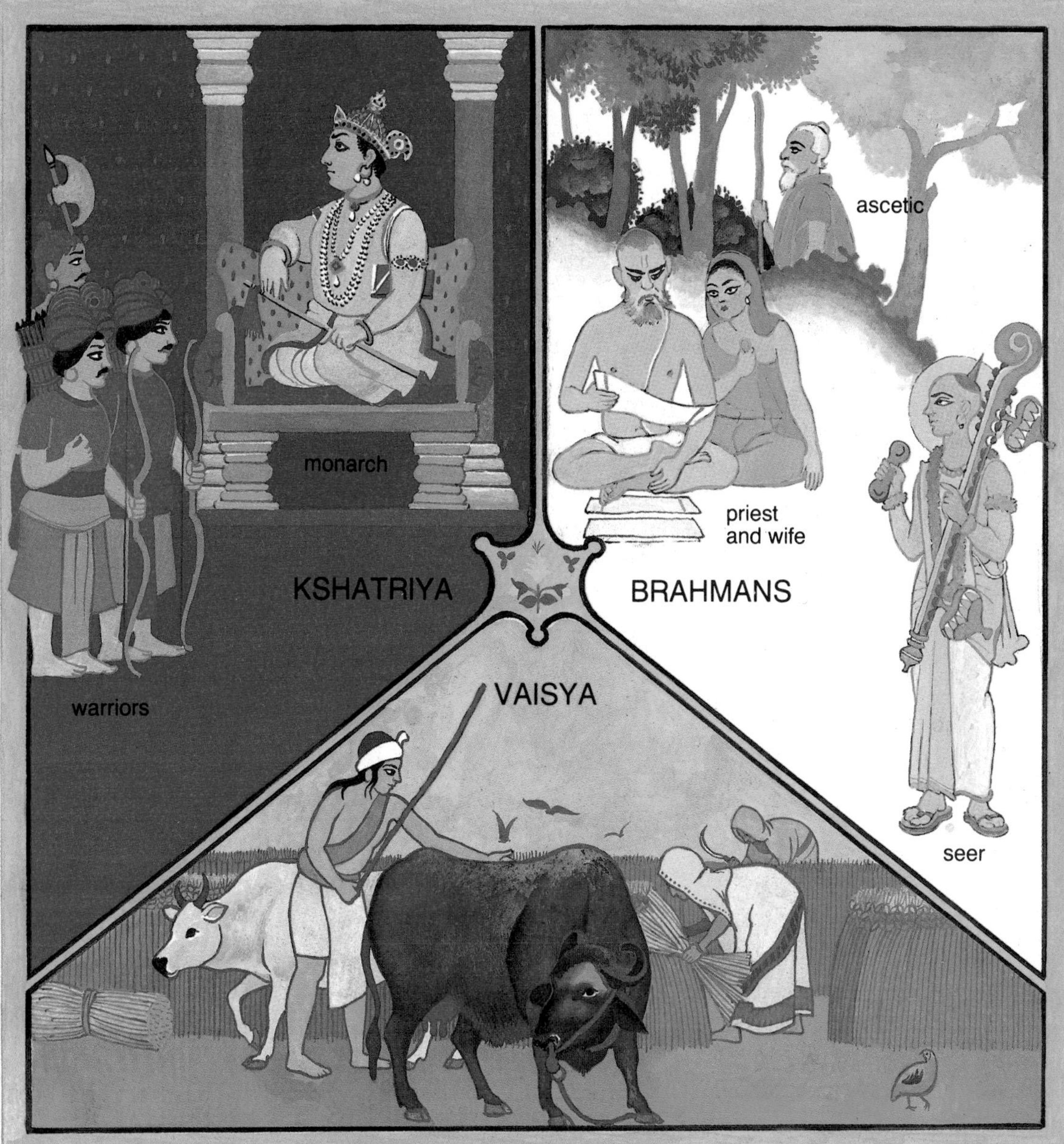

The Indo-European tribes that settled in India were divided into three main social groups, commonly called castes. The Brahmans were the priests, who maintained relationships with the world of the deities for the whole community. Among them were the rishi, or seers, and the ascetics. (Ascetics practiced rigid self-denial as a religious act.) The Kshatriya had the military power. This caste consisted of warriors, groups of which were lead by a raja, or monarch. The Vaisya had the economic power because they farmed the land, raised the cattle, and eventually took on trading businesses. Each caste had its own typical color: the Brahmans wore white, the Kshatriya wore red, and the Vaisya wore yellow.

struction materials, no trace of the dwellings remains today.

The Vedic Society

The social organization of the Indo-European tribes is usually called Vedic. This organization is named for the tribe's sacred texts, the Vedas, and is entirely based on the truth revealed in them. In fact, the name *Veda* comes from the sanscrit word *vid,* which means "to know." The Vedas are a collection of supposedly divinely revealed truths, gathered and ordered by the old seers (rishi). The text of the Veda is practically the only true cultural treasure of this period (1500-1000 B.C.) that remains.

As the Indo-European tribes settled on the Indian continent, they created a rural world. The basic structure of this world was the village. Inside the village, the family was the main structure around which all everyday activities revolved. Work in the fields was often done cooperatively, and the economy was almost completely based on farming. Religion had a major role in Vedic society, and the priests held important social positions. The Vedic religion was Hinduism.

The Division into Castes

A typical feature of the Vedic world was the so-called caste system. By this system, society was divided into three major groups, each one with various rights and duties. Actually, the word *caste* does not belong to the Indian tradition. It was created by the Portuguese colonizers who reached India in A.D. 1600. The Sanscrit word for what is called caste is *jati,* which means "birth" or "origin," stressing the fact that a person's caste is determined by birth.

During the early times of Vedic society, castes were not yet closed. Instead, the classes were based on the three basic social activities: religion (priests), offense and defense (warriors), and sustaining the population (farmers, herders, artisans). But as time passed, around 1000 B.C., the class system became more rigid and shifted into a caste system. In this system, birth determines a person's caste once and forever, and it cannot be changed. Marriages are permitted only within the same caste, and the offspring automatically belong to their parents' caste. The three principal castes are: the priests (Brahmans), who maintain relationships with the world of deities; the warriors and monarchs (Kshatriya) who tend to war and government; and the merchants and farmers (Vaisya).

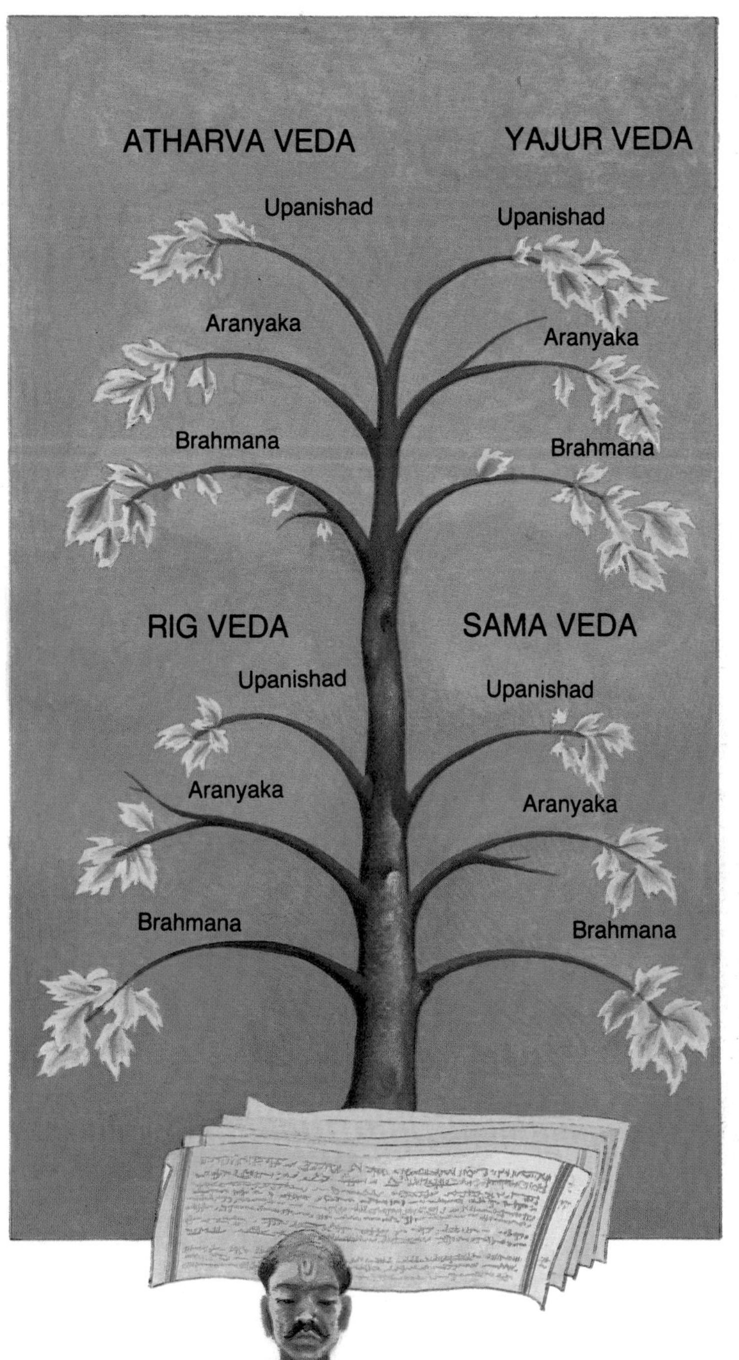

Above: The Indo-European religion in India was based on four sacred books called the Vedas. The word *veda* is a Sanscrit word meaning "knowledge." In this drawing, the Vedas are shown like a large tree. The branches represent the subgroups which comprise the four Vedas and the subdivision within each Veda. The Veda text is contained on typical rectangular sheets. Some were ornate with decorations, and sometimes the wealthiest Brahmans owned sheets with writing in gold letters. *Below:* A young Brahman sits in the typical position of concentration and meditation.

INDIA: HINDUISM

The Four Veda

The first three books of the Veda—Rig Veda, Sama Veda, and Yajur Veda—preserve the religious, philosophical, and literary history of the Indo-European people. The fourth Veda, the Atharva Veda, was later added to these three. Even today, however, some Brahmans do not consider this Veda sacred.

The Vedas, and particularly the Rig Veda, are considered Hinduism's most sacred books. The teachings contained in the Vedas, however, are not like those of the Bible. In that book, God practically dictates to the prophets the message for the chosen people. Nor are they like the epic narrations of Greek mythology, where the narrators were poets. The rishi (or seer) is neither prophet nor poet. He does not need a chosen people nor a listening crowd. His is a personal experience, which occurs under certain mental and physical conditions. It is what is called sruti, or the revelation of knowledge. According to myth, this occurred four times corresponding to the four great periods into which the Vedic Indians divide life in the world. These are: the golden age (kritayuga), in which the Rig Veda was revealed; the silver age (tretayuga), in which the Yajur Veda was revealed; the bronze age (dvaparayuga), in which the Atharva Veda was revealed; and the iron age (kaliyuga) in which the Sama Veda was revealed. It can be said that each Veda reveals a particular aspect of religious life.

Hindu Deities

Hinduism is polytheistic, which means it has many gods. Most gods, or deities, are males with the exception of Aditi, the mother of the gods. Some of the main gods are Indra, Varuna, Agni, Surya, and Yama. Indra is the master of the gods, the supreme god of the heavens. He is the symbol of warriors and of the Indo-European heroes. He protects the Indo-European

Sacrificial offerings to the gods were very important in Hinduism. Usually, the Brahmans would offer the main sacrifices, but some of them were offered by the monarch. The most well-known and spectacular sacrifice was the "sacrifice of the horse." In this ritual, the king, assisted by court Brahmans and knights, would bless a horse, and then set it free to roam the kingdom. After a year, the animal was captured, richly adorned, and harnessed to a chariot. The horse then pulled the chariot, with the king riding in it, in a procession. At the end of the ceremony, the horse was sacrificed.

peoples from their enemies and keeps order in the world by killing demons. Like the Roman god Jupiter, Indra is the master of lightning and uses it as a weapon to battle his enemies. Varuna, like Uranus of Greek mythology, is the supreme god of waters. He is the keeper of the Supreme Law, or dharma, which he himself established in the beginning. He has unlimited visual powers; the sun is his eye, and he knows the destiny of every person. Agni is the god of fire. He was an extremely powerful deity in the ancient world, where fire was an important element of life. The origins of the cult of Agni go back to prehistoric religions. This god was considered the central symbol of farming life. Surya is the god of the sun. His cult was among the most important for people of ancient times. Surya is the great eye in the sky which sees everything and surveys gods and mortals. Yama, the god of death, is also the father of the human race.

THE PRINCIPAL GODS OF HINDUISM

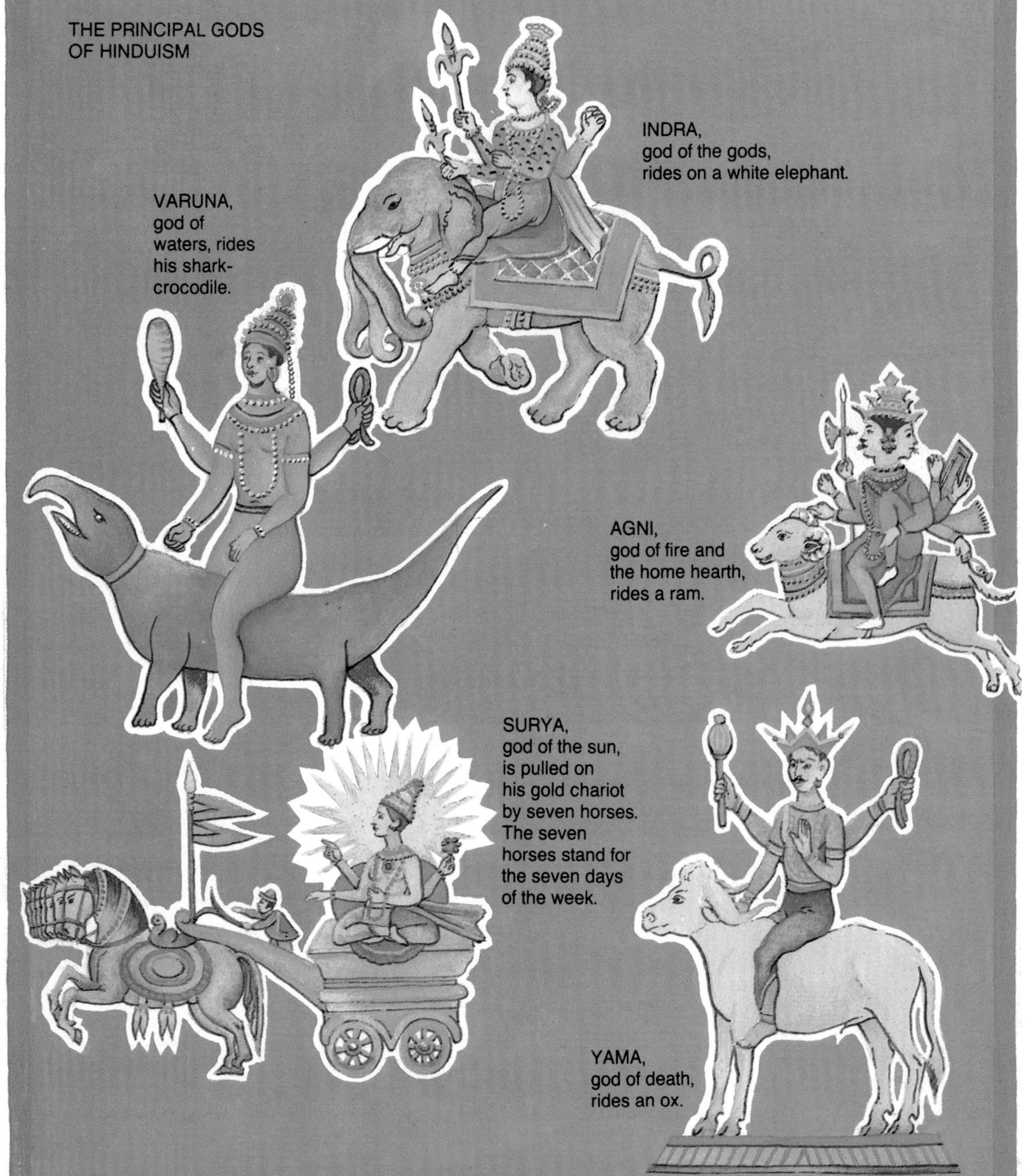

INDRA, god of the gods, rides on a white elephant.

VARUNA, god of waters, rides his shark-crocodile.

AGNI, god of fire and the home hearth, rides a ram.

SURYA, god of the sun, is pulled on his gold chariot by seven horses. The seven horses stand for the seven days of the week.

YAMA, god of death, rides an ox.

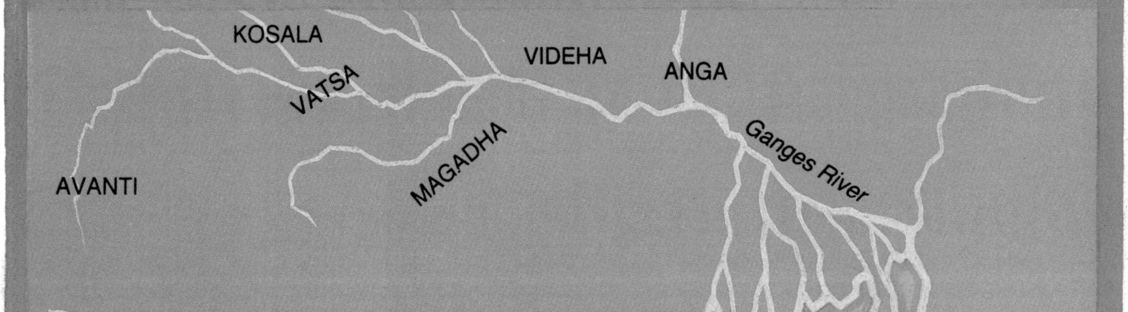

KOSALA

VATSA

VIDEHA

ANGA

AVANTI

MAGADHA

Ganges River

The End of the Vedic Period

From around 1000 to 500 B.C. the Indo-European populations (Aryans) of the Vedic culture spread rapidly. They pushed further east until they had conquered nearly all of the territories along the upper Ganges in northern India. Knowledge of this period comes mainly from the sacred texts of the Brahmana and the Upanishad. The Aryan populations grew, and the battles became full scale wars. The occupied territories became kingdoms, though many were quite small and tribal. The most powerful among these were Kosala, Magadha, Avanti, and Vatsa. These kingdoms had permanent capital cities and the beginnings of an administrative system. As the authority of the king and his court grew, the power of the tribal assemblies lessened.

The villages were still the most common settlements, but cities were also beginning to develop. In addition to gold and copper, the Aryans of the late Vedic period knew how to work with tin, lead, silver, and especially iron. The farming of cereal crops flourished. Occupations became more specialized.

BUDDHISM AND JAINISM IN INDIA

The Life of Buddha

Around 500 B.C., northwestern India was having a deep religious crisis. The Vedic world had lost most of its energy. Religion was often reduced to a formal routine which the Brahman caste carried out without any enthusiasm.

In reaction, the Indian society witnessed the birth of several preachings intended to renew the spirit of religion. The most important of these new religious trends was Buddhism. Its founder was Gautama Siddhartha, the king of a small realm in northern India.

Gautama Siddhartha was born around 560 B.C. in Kapilavastu and was raised with all the honors due to a young prince. His family, fearing that contact with the world would disturb him, kept the boy secure from all of life's difficulties. He passed the first twenty-nine years of his life within his father's royal palace. Completely ignorant of what was happening in the outside world, Gautama grew healthy and happy. When he was of age, he married Jasodhara, a girl of noble heritage. Soon they had a son.

One day, curiosity took the prince beyond the walls of the royal palace. In the city streets, Gautama suddenly faced the daily reality of human life. He saw a spectacle to which he was not accustomed and one which he had not even dreamed existed. He met a sick man and learned

To the left: **(1)** Prince Gautama Siddhartha, the Buddha, lived and taught in India in the fifth century B.C. **(2)** Before he was born, Gautama's mother dreamed he entered her womb in the form of a white elephant. **(3)** The young prince sits in the garden of the royal palace of the father. **(4)** The prince meets with an old man, a sick man, and a dead man. These experiences reveal to Gautama the suffering and limits of life. An ascetic shows him the path of spiritual search which Gautama, after taking on the poor cloak of the monks, will follow until reaching enlightenment. **(5)** After a search of many years, Gautama attains enlightenment under a pipal tree. **(6)** In the Park of the Gazelle in Sarnath, Gautama gives his first public speech. In it, he explains the doctrine of the Four Noble Truths: Suffering, the Causes of Suffering, the Means to Overcome Suffering, and the Righteousness of These Means. **(7)** The Four Noble Truths are represented by a wheel divided into four sections.

This colossal statue captures the Buddha at the moment of his death (Parinirvana) in 483 B.C. The statue is at Polonnaruva on the island of Sri Lanka.

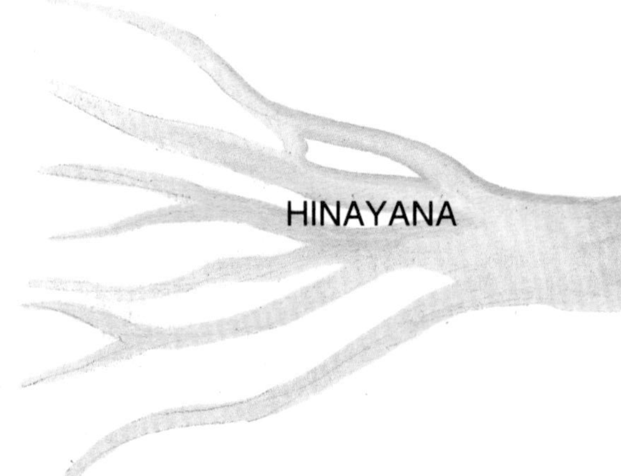

To the left: Three important aspects of Buddhism, often called the three jewels, are: the Buddha, the principle of enlightenment; the Dharma, the path which leads to enlightenment; and the Sangha, the community of the faithful.

that the body could get sick. Next he met an old man and had to face the pains of old age. Finally, he saw a dead man being carried to the grave and knew the tragedy of death.

This sudden revelation of human suffering disturbed the prince. But then he saw an ascetic go by. The man was old in age but had a serene expression on his face. At that moment, Gautama Siddhartha decided to abandon the palace and his family and follow the spiritual path. He set off at once in search of an enlightenment that would free him from life's suffering. His spiritual search was long, hard, and lasted many years. Finally one day, as Gautama meditated under a tree in the village of Uruvela (today called Bodh-Gaya), his mind opened, and he attained enlightenment. Others heard of Gautama's experience and began to call him Buddha, which means "the Enlightened." The Buddha spent the rest of his life preaching and trying to teach others how to overcome suffering.

The Four Noble Truths

The heart of Buddhist preaching is contained in the Buddha's first public speech. This speech, which Buddha gave after attaining enlightenment, is known as the speech of the Four Noble Truths. The first of these truths is that life is suffering. The second says that the cause of suffering is mental confusion, which causes people to become attached to worldly things. The third states that suffering can be ended by removing the causes. The fourth reveals the eight-stage path by which it can be ended.

JAPAN

The Spread of Buddhism

Soon after the death of the Buddha, the Buddhist community divided into many schools and currents. Buddhism spread in India and was the principal religion of the country for about a thousand years. Between the fourth and the first century B.C., Buddhism reached Sri Lanka and became the main religion of the island. About the same time, the religion spread both to the southeast (in Burma and the Indochina peninsula) and to the north, reaching the Himalayan region, Tibet, China, Korea, and Japan. It also spread to the west, to present day Afghanistan, but here the arrival of Islamic populations (around A.D. 800) wiped out all traces of Buddhism.

Mahavira, the master of Jainism

Jainism

Jainism originated through a chain of spiritual masters (Tirthamkara) that goes back to very ancient times. The main organizer of this religion was the last great master, Mahavira. Mahavira lived and preached at the same time as the Buddha. Jainism does not believe in a creator god, gives great importance to ethics, and proclaims that inner enlightenment is possible through a combination of faith in the masters, knowledge of the way the human mind works, and proper moral conduct. Jainists must respect five vows: sincerity, a nonviolent way of life, refraining from stealing, refraining from incorrect behavior, and refraining from greed. Jainism never spread out of north-central India. It was formally organized in the fifth century B.C., had its golden age between A.D. 300 and 800, and then slowly declined. Today, the Jainist religion numbers about two million followers.

The Jainist ascetics go naked to show their complete poverty. Some followers even cover their mouths with cloths to avoid swallowing insects, in order to keep their vows of nonviolence toward all living things.

Below: Buddhism is divided into three periods, called the three vehicles, which correspond to the three stages of the spiritual path. The Hinayana is the first period, in which the basics of the religious practice are laid. During this time, followers withdraw in order to know themselves and improve. The Mahayana is the second period. In this period, after having grown better, the followers open themselves to others in order to help them. The Vajrayana, often kept secret, is the period in which the most difficult rituals and meditations are performed.

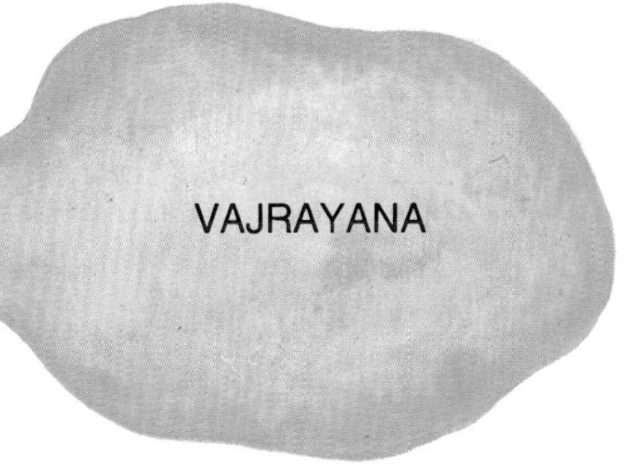

This drawing shows the burial of a nomadic leader. In this scene, the burial chamber has already been prepared with wood-covered walls.

This fragment of a felt saddle blanket is decorated with a galloping moose. (500 B.C.)

This gold plaque of an animal of prey was found in the territory west of Altai.

This wood pendant in the shape of a human head, once decorated a horse harness.

THE PEOPLES OF THE STEPPES OF CENTRAL ASIA

Agriculture and the Shift to Nomadism

The populations inhabiting the huge stretch of steppe covering the Asian continent north of India and northwest of China had gradually learned to domesticate animals. Still more slowly, they had learned to farm the land. About 2000 B.C., people started living in stable settlements in houses that were partially underground. At the time, the steppe was farmed from the Urals to the Tien Shan valleys. Suddenly, around 900 B.C., the situation changed. For reasons still unknown, the steppe populations abandoned their villages and their farming habits and became nomadic. In a very short time, they extensively colonized the steppes with livestock.

Politics, Economy, and Art

In the west, the steppe nomads moved slowly toward the Iranian plateau. The Mediums went first. They were followed by the Persians and then the Parthians. In the east, the nomads clashed with the Chinese Empire. Despite their nomadic ways, the various populations had similar life-styles. Many groups raised cattle, which were a symbol of wealth and social importance. Meat and dairy products then became staple foods for these people, and pelts became important trade items. But even weapons, harnesses, and ornaments were similar in the different groups. Trading became important to all groups as a means of obtaining necessary goods, but raiding was also frequent.

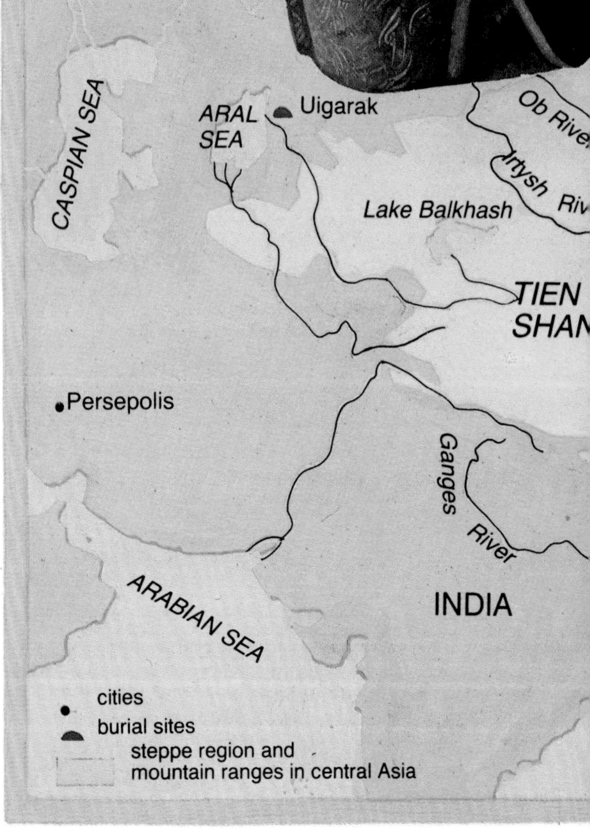

Below: This cross section shows that the ground around a burial mound remains frozen in both winter and summer.

Below: A mound in Pazyryk in the Altai region.

The Cooling System of the Tombs

In 1927, when archaeologists began to excavate the Altai mounds, they found their contents very well preserved. Human bodies and even perishable artifacts (felt, leather, other fabrics, and wood) had been preserved by ice.

The drawings here explain why the temperature inside the mounds always remained below the freezing point. Once the tomb was closed, dirt was thrown over it. Next, a mound of stones up to several feet high was placed on top. Since the funerals were held in the cold season, the soil underneath the mound soon froze. During the summer, these stones allowed air circulation but kept the sun's heat from defrosting the underlying ground. During the winter, the cold stones would further lower the temperature inside the burial chamber. Because of the constant low temperature, water and humidity in the tomb were turned into ice before they could damage its contents.

These people owned few possessions, all of which were easily transported. However, even these objects were richly decorated with plant patterns, animal representations, battle scenes, or a few human figures. The patterns were basically outlines. A few lines would define a profile or frontal image and were enough to convey the meaning of the decoration and a sense of great power.

The Burial Rituals

By this time, ceremonies marking important events were very much a part of people's lives. There was often great detail and pageantry involved. This was true of the burial ritual, especially that of a leader. From the many tombs discovered, scholars are able to describe such a funeral. First, the dead body was embalmed. In this state, it was kept until the beginning of spring or autumn. At the chosen moment, a rectangular pit of up to 23 feet (7 m) deep was dug. Inside it, a hut was built with larch logs covering its floor and ceiling. The coffin was placed inside the hut, along with rugs, vases, stringed instruments, weapons, and tables on which to offer sacrifices. After the burial, a great funeral banquet would take place.

The Religion

The people believed the universe was watched over by the creator god Tangri. Life on earth and human destiny depended on this god, who was well known throughout the Asian steppe. The universe itself existed on three levels: the Sky, the Earth, and the Underworld. These three levels were connected by a central axis, and passage from one level to the next was possible.

The person capable of passing from one level to another was the shaman. The shaman used this ability to intervene for the community at particularly difficult moments, such as when there was illness or when game was scarce. With rituals accompanied by drumming, imitations of animal calls, and the smoking of hemp, the shaman would descend into the Underworld or ascend into the Sky. Upon his return, the shaman would tell the people the will of the gods.

This reconstruction is of a city during the Shang period. The palaces for the administration are built very differently from the traditional Neolithic houses.

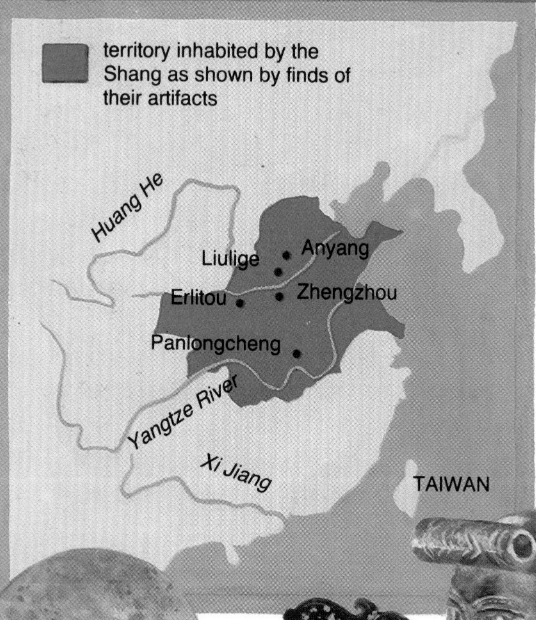

territory inhabited by the Shang as shown by finds of their artifacts

Huang He
Liulige
Anyang
Erlitou
Zhengzhou
Panlongcheng
Yangtze River
Xi Jiang
TAIWAN

China Enters the Bronze Age: The Shang Dynasty

The First Dynasty: Myth or Reality?

About 100 B.C., the Chinese historian Sima Qian wrote the first major history of China. This history of the Chinese dynasties illustrates the evolution of the early Chinese societies. At first, during the herding period, people were mainly sustained by animals. Then, a farming period began. After that came the reign of the three kings Huang, Yao, and Shun. Succeeding them was Yu the Great, who is thought to have founded the first royal Chinese dynasty, that of the Hsia (Xia), around 2200 B.C.

This first dynasty has been considered imaginary for a long time, like other myths on the world's origin. However, evidence of its existence has been found. In Shaanxi and in the Henan region, some very rough gray pottery has been found. Its complex shape suggests that it was the product of a society between the Neolithic period and the Bronze Age.

The Shang Dynasty

Around 1500 B.C., China entered the Bronze Age with the Shang dynasty. Several elements distinguish this civilization, and knowledge of it

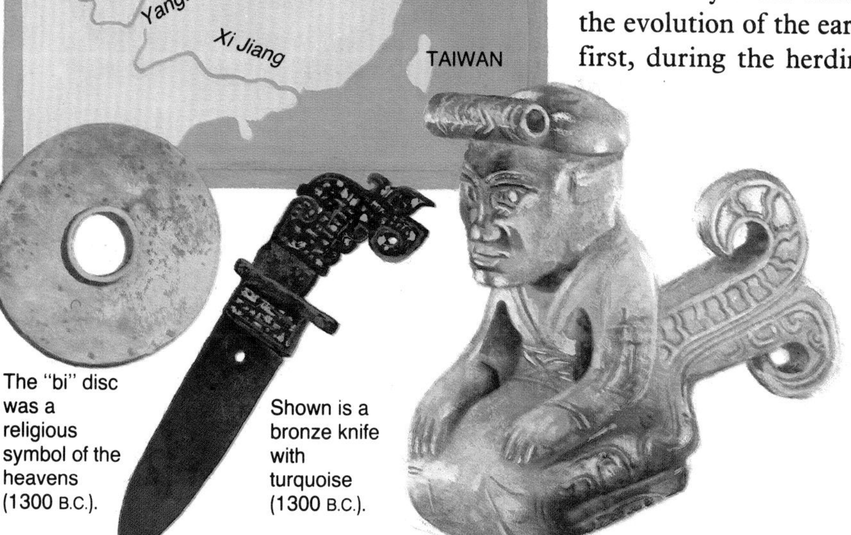

The "bi" disc was a religious symbol of the heavens (1300 B.C.).

Shown is a bronze knife with turquoise (1300 B.C.).

This small jade figurine is the oldest known representation of a government official. This figurine wears official clothing and kneels in a revering posture.

In a foundry, workers pour melted bronze into a mold. Another worker is refining the decoration on a piece that has been taken from its mold. In the foreground, a large vase, molded in one piece, is used to cook sacrificial food. (Shang dynasty, 1100 B.C.)

comes easier because of the gradual appearance of writing. The first urban settlements rose where the various capitals of the dynasty were to develop. In one such settlement in Erlitou, the buildings were halfway between those of the Neolithic villages and those of the imperial cities still to come.

Today, several examples of this kind of town still exist. Such a place was surrounded by dirt walls. Its buildings were on terraces and had walls made of hay mixed with dry mud. Besides these imposing buildings, which housed government representatives, another feature of the Shang dynasty was its concept of death, funerals, and tombs. The royal tombs were especially beautiful.

During the Shang dynasty, bronze forging was developed. Many items for both daily use and for religious rituals were made of metal. These included farming tools, weapons, and vases for cooking or for heating alcohol. The decorative patterns were at first simple outlines like those used on Neolithic pottery. With time, the decorations became more detailed, and many showed a mythological influence. Mythological animals such as the serpent, dragon, or taotie glutton (which devours its prey without swallowing it) and familiar ones began to appear on the pottery. Similar decorations are also found on objects made of other material, such as ivory and jade. Jade, which was believed to have magical powers, was used to make bi disks.

The Shang dynasty, which included thirty-one kings, eventually lost its power. With each generation, the kings became more corrupt and were not able to "maintain a balance beneath the sky." New clans took control, changing the name of the dynasty to avoid bad luck. They named it Yin, which means "powerful, prosperous." This period began with King Pan Keng (around 1300 B.C.) but decline continued, and the Shang (or Yin) dynasty disappeared on a still-uncertain date.

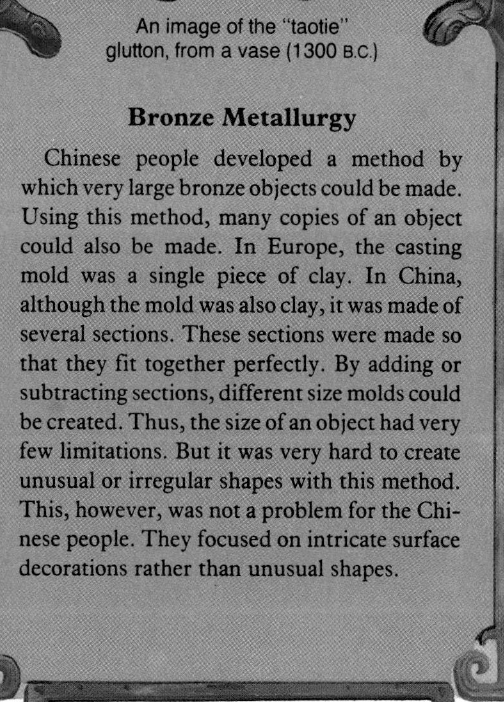

An image of the "taotie" glutton, from a vase (1300 B.C.)

Bronze Metallurgy

Chinese people developed a method by which very large bronze objects could be made. Using this method, many copies of an object could also be made. In Europe, the casting mold was a single piece of clay. In China, although the mold was also clay, it was made of several sections. These sections were made so that they fit together perfectly. By adding or subtracting sections, different size molds could be created. Thus, the size of an object had very few limitations. But it was very hard to create unusual or irregular shapes with this method. This, however, was not a problem for the Chinese people. They focused on intricate surface decorations rather than unusual shapes.

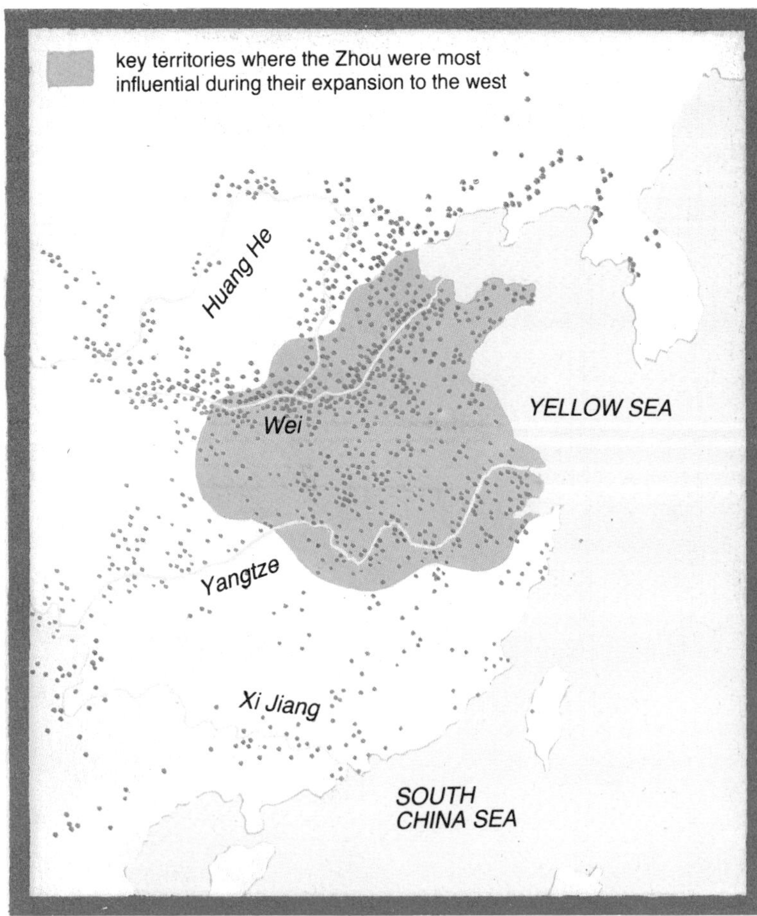

This map marks the locations of the fortified cities during the Zhou period. Most of the construction work took place in Zhou territories along their communication routes.

THE EMPIRE MOVES WEST: THE ZHOU DYNASTY

The Realm of the Zhou

When the "warrior king" Wu took power from the last king of the Shang dynasty, he established his headquarters in a region further west, the actual Shaanxi region. He proclaimed himself the protector of the civilization that was blossoming in the valley and along the rivers. He did not use violence with the conquered peoples. In fact, many aristocrats were able to preserve their economic, social, and even political way of life under the Zhou. For this reason, the early Zhou reign seemed to continue in the tradition of the Shang dynasty, with which the Zhou had previously formed tight bonds through cooperation in war.

In order to gain power in the provinces, the Zhou did not conquer the territories. On the contrary, they sent government representatives to these territories. Often representatives were members of the royal family. They would settle in the new region with their families, their administrative staffs, priests of their ancestral religion, and their seers. In this way, numerous cities, called cheng cities, were developed.

Thanks to the discovery of the Fengchu palace in the Shaanxi region, archaeologists now have a clear image of the administrative settlements from which the various regional capitals developed. The palace of Fengchu was composed of a close network of buildings and adjoining rooms surrounded by a rectangular enclosure. It is estimated to have been built about 1000 B.C. The buildings were made of wood and cemented with a clay, stone, and hay mixture. They were placed around a large building used for ceremonies.

Bronze Objects Old and New

Besides the daily tools and ritual vases, a middle category of bronze objects evolved. These were the objects that kings or other important people had made in honor of an alliance or a wedding. They were highly symbolic artifacts, inscribed with details of the honored event. During the Shang period, these inscriptions were limited to two or three characters. With the Zhou, as many as five hundred characters described the circumstances of the

Shown is a clash between a Zhou army and a group of nomads on the border. Starting about 800 B.C., the power of the Zhou kings was threatened by these invading nomads and by the growing power of local lords.

To the left: In the court of a provincial palace, an administrator receives a concession of land. In the last few years, several cities of the Zhou period have been discovered. They are similar to the one found in Qishan, which inspired this drawing.

Each territory had its own currency. The currency was made of bronze, and the most common shapes were **(1)** the hoe and **(2)** the knife. During the Zhou period, bronze objects were made not only for royal ceremonies, but also for all the occasions which marked the lifetime of all important people: alliances, weddings, and land deals. The quality of the bronze objects became more and more refined. As seen here, **(3)** a bell, **(4)** a ritual vase, **(5)** a buffalo, and **(6)** an elephant have been richly decorated.

pact and the intent of those who had sealed it.

For daily use, very simple gray ceramic vessels were used. They were shaped much like those of the Shang period. But the Zhou potters did not have the skills of the earlier potters. They had lost the secret to making kaolin. Kaolin, or china clay, is a pure white clay still widely used to make fine pottery. Potters of the Shang period had somehow learned to make and use kaolin. With it, they were producing finely decorated pottery using the same patterns as those used for bronze vases.

Back to the East: The So-Called Eastern Zhou Period

There are still doubts among scholars regarding the real power of the Zhou. Undoubtedly, their power had weakened by the time the kings moved the capital back to the Henan region in 771 B.C. They too had fallen victim to the warlike nomads coming from the west. These invaders were attracted by the wealth of the plains and the foothill regions.

But this was not the only reason for the Zhou's loss of power. Over time, the bond between the Zhou and their administrators had weakened. The administrators became more independent, and the prestige of the king, who traditionally had been the only intermediary between the Earth and the Sky, between people and their ancestors, was now missing. Political disruption and the fall of the royal cult went hand in hand. The cities and the surrounding regions turned into small independent states. Trading and exchanges continued between the provinces, but each was now ruled independently.

CHANGES IN THE FIRST MILLENNIUM B.C.

Great Divisions of the Period

When the Zhou kings moved their capital to the Henan region, they were certainly trying to escape the invading nomads. But, perhaps without realizing it, they had also opened up the development of a new technology—that of iron. Although the Zhou dynasty continued until about 250 B.C., it gradually became less and less important. During this long period, two successive stages occurred in Chinese society. The first is the Spring and Autumn period (Chunqiu, 770-485 B.C.). The second is the epoch of the Warring States period (Zhanguo, 485-221 B.C.), whose name reflects the instability of the times.

During the Spring and Autumn period, China was divided into many small princedoms, each being independent. They developed either trading or hostile relationships, spurred by a lack of federal institutions. The government, in fact, was in the hands of the aristocracy (various royal clans), well apart from the farmer and servant classes.

Soon after it had been segmented, the Chinese territory began to reunite. Starting around 500 B.C., a new process of unification began. The smaller states fell into the hands of the more powerful, until, during the period of the Warring States, only seven main states survived. These were: Yan, Zhao, Jin, Qin, Chu, Shu, and Qi. These states originated from the unification of ancient and sometimes-powerful princedoms which were rapidly conquered or annexed. The kingdoms of Yue, Wi, and Han, for example, were conquered by Chu. The state of Lu, home of Confucius, was annexed to the powerful Qi. Most of the wealth of the Qi state came from exploiting the forests in the mountain areas of the Shandong region and from maritime resources, mainly salt. Recent archaeological excavations in the areas of small states such as Zhongshan and Zeng, which are briefly mentioned in Chinese histories, have been surprisingly successful.

Political and Economic Life

The frequency of trade, and even more importantly, the frequency of war, brought changes to the political world. These things also triggered the rise of a new social class: that of the masters. The masters were counselors to the princes, nomadic philosophers, and dispensers of professional advice. They were ready to sell their services to those who could pay.

A new sense of relationships and alliances began to develop. It was based on subtle strategic and economic balancing acts between the various princedoms. The states were constantly in conflict over border contentions and were ever ready to reclaim the wealth of neighboring states.

Wealth, especially in the central countries such as the Chu, was abundant. Growth in consumer goods came along with development of complex metal and lacquer techniques (metals were encrusted with all possible kinds of material). The process of storage of grains and fruit also improved, along with their variety. Such change took place gradually and at different rates in the different regions. Still it shows an improvement in farming methods. This was partly due to the variety of tools now used by the farmers. Some of these had been inherited from the Neolithic age but were highly improved by the use of bronze and later of iron. The iron tools were cast, not wrought. They were cast using methods which bronze casters had been employing for about a thousand years.

The use of coins, already common in the Zhou period, increased widely in this period. Bronze, which was considered a noble metal, was often used for coins. The coins varied in size and weight from state to state, but they would often circulate between different princedoms. Like the coins of the previous period, they imitated the shapes of farming tools (the goods exchanged were grains). In some states, a round bronze coin with a square hole in the center was used. Coins of this kind were to become the official currency of the empire.

The Evolution of Chinese Society

Passing from the Neolithic to the metal age, Chinese society underwent major changes. The feminine element lost importance in the social environment, and the male element became predominant. At the same time, the first states, with political power over a certain territory, developed. Metal technology favored those who knew how to find, transport, and melt metals. An ever-growing knowledge of metals made way for better tools, thus increasing the productivity of the land. Good tools were also indispensable for the great digging works connected with the construction of buildings or the regulation of waterways.

In this way, a small number of clans and families obtained power, and walled cities developed. These were the residences of the king or of one of his representatives, who lived there with various ministers, protected by an army. The walled city in which they lived separated them from the common people.

Iron working in melting ovens begins. This permits very large pieces to be made. *To the right:* This mold was used for the manufacture of scythes.

To the right and below: This colored lacquer drum and duck came from southern China. The use of lacquer, made from a vegetable sap, spread through China in the fifth century B.C.

Fights between the Chinese states were frequent. Battles were also fought from chariots. Crossbows, made of wood and bronze, effectively took the place of other bows. They came into use around the end of the Warring States period and were to become common in the Han.

To the left: This decorative piece, made of bronze and encrusted with gold, came from the tomb of King Cuo in Zhongshan (400 B.C.).

To the left: Shown is a large bronze basin, set on wheels, dating back to the Wu princedom (600 to 500 B.C.).

Below is the reconstruction of a huge mausoleum, or burial tomb, for the royal burials in the Zhongshan region (400 B.C.). This is an example of the monumental complexes which were built in this period.

This bronze emblem was a symbol of royal power in the Zhongshan region.

Trade develops, and trading centers multiply. *To the left:* A typical village market where multicolored glass beads (inset) were highly prized.

This gold deer was made by the northern steppe populations, neighbors of the princedoms.

THE TRADITIONAL CHINESE RELIGION

The Earth, the Sky, the People, and Their Ancestors

The city was considered the symbol of the world ruled by the king. Beyond that, it was a symbol of the whole universe. For this reason, each season the king would move from one part of it to another, imitating a journey through his territories. The city was also the place where the king celebrated his rituals, communicating with the Sky and obtaining his power from it. The Sky, on the other hand, also needed humankind: the Earth (square) and the Sky (round) could never remain in balance were it not for people. People were considered the axis of the universe, and the king was, by definition, the heart of humankind.

The sense of sacred is seen even more clearly in the rural cults, especially in the cult of the ancestors. The ancestors of the Chinese race had a great deal of experience, especially experience with death. They were worshipped with special ceremonies, sacrifices, and banquets in the temple dedicated to them. Initially, only the ancestors of the royal family and of the most important families were worshipped.

Death and Burials

Death was considered a repetition of life as it had been on the earth. In fact, at the moment of death, some souls (each individual was believed to have several souls) would stay inside the body of the dead. This allowed the body to lead another existence, similar to the one it had on earth.

For this reason, important people, kings in particular, were buried with great pomp, enclosed in several coffins which were covered by a sarcophagus, or stone coffin. The sarcophagus was placed inside a burial pit of compacted dirt, with walls covered by wooden boards. Objects necessary to the lives of the dead were placed inside small, adjoining rooms and on benches around the sarcophagus. These were objects that the dead had possessed during life, or other objects especially made for the funeral rituals.

What horrifies many people is the custom of human sacrifice as part of the burial ritual. But it is logical to the thinking of that time. The king needed women, servants, and companions to attend him. Among those usually sacrificed was a man—generally accompanied by a dog—who was placed underneath the coffins in a small room. The tomb was in the middle, with steps on three sides on which soldiers, killed on the spot, stood guard. The royal coach, with sacrificed horses and chariot drivers, rested on the slanted platform used to lower the sarcophagus into the tomb. Not far from the royal tomb, other burial sites could contain other coaches and beheaded war prisoners, as well as ministers or friends of the dead.

Only the very important people were given all this honor. In many tombs of common people, the dead were accompanied only by some ceramics. The habit of costly sacrifices, typical of the Bronze Age, disappeared very rapidly. Starting from the Warring States period (475-221 B.C.), wooden statuettes and ceramics started taking the place of human sacrifices.

Divination

The art of consulting the gods or the ancestors in order to know their opinion on particular issues was very important in China. This practice was called divination. The most ancient divination practices date back to the Neolithic age, but only during the Bronze Age did they become well known. The first examples of Chinese writing are associated with them (see the chart in the following chapter). Writing was used to note the questions asked of the gods or ancestors, and especially their answers.

Several kinds of divination were used, but the development of writing corresponded to the beginning of divination using animal bones. This kind of divination was based on the fact that some flat bones, such as deer or cow shoulder bones, or turtle shells, would crack in intricate patterns when touched with a hot stick. The stick was applied to a special spot on the bone which had been lightly carved before the ceremony. The diviners then studied the network of cracks and found answers to the people's questions in it. The questions asked, together with the answers obtained, were written on the bones at the end of the ritual.

Gods and ancestors were questioned on all the major issues. Eventually, it was agreed to have divinations every ten days. These bones and scales were neatly preserved in special hidden pits inside the palaces. The people used this written collection of questions and answers like a legal code. Scholars first discovered these oracle bones, as they are called, near the tombs of Anyang in this century.

Above: The royal tomb at Anyang is seen from above. Numerous people, such as soldiers, prisoners, servants, and friends, were killed to accompany the king into the underworld. They were placed in various places and postures throughout the tomb.

Opposite page, top: This funeral scene was inspired by the paintings on the Mawangdui silk-cloth. The richly decorated sarcophagus is in the middle of the scene. In the foreground and background are several vases for the ritual offerings. Also in the background is a long row of bells.

To the right: To get an answer to his question, the diviner touched a large turtle shell with a burning hot stick. Such shells were obtained from animals raised especially for divination purposes and killed during a sacred ceremony. *Insert:* This is how a shell looked after the ceremony. The writing was carved into the shell by the priest, to record the questions asked and the answers received.

The Mawangdui Silk-Cloth

This cloth represents the earliest-known example of Chinese painting on silk. It covered the coffin of a woman who died in the second century B.C. The main figures on the cloth are as follows (from bottom to top): aquatic creatures, the funeral ceremony, the celestial veil carried by sirens, the union of the Yin and Yang dragons, the dead in the underworld, the sky supported by a bat, two wise men, some dragons, the sun with a jay, a fruit tree *(to the right)*, and the moon inhabited by a toad and a hare *(to the left)*.

To the left, bottom: The painting on the Mawangdui cloth is very detailed. This is how the Chinese imagined a dead woman in the underworld, accompanied by her servants. Also on this cloth are the Yin and Yang dragons. The union of these dragons creates all living beings. In the center, a bat supports the sky.

Below: The Mawangdui silk-cloth is pictured.

The Classical Age of Literature

"Classic" Chinese Thought

During the Zhou dynasty and the Warring States period, a major political fragmentation occurred in China. This resulted in the creation of many different communities. In these newly formed, independent communities, the Chinese culture experienced a great flowering of the human mind. It was a period of new expression. Philosophers traveled through these communities, each spreading a new school of thought. Because of their great numbers, the group was collectively known as the "Hundred Schools." But from this group emerged several important philosophers such as Confucius, Mencius, Lao-Tsu, Hsun-Tsu, and Han-Feitze.

This bronze incense burner comes from the Mancheng tomb. The top part represents the mountain of the immortals, which is the Daoist paradise. The wise men who were able to reach the mountain without passing through death dwell there.

Until very recently, the thoughts of these philosophers were known only through what public officials had written about them around the beginning of the Christian era. At that time, historians had taken on the task of researching and organizing the written history of China. For many centuries, the historical works had been collectively referred to by the term *literature.* The group included any text of some moral, intellectual, or scientific value. The notable collection of writings was classified in the first Chinese bibliographic volume contained in the *History of the Han.* The *History of the Han* was written in the first century B.C. This bibliography, which was later reorganized, was to be the reference point of all Chinese knowledge to the present time.

The Thoughts of Confucius

The structure of ancient Chinese philosophical and learned thought was based on teachings of five books known as the *Five Classics.* Early scholars credited these works to the great philosopher Confucius (about 551-479 B.C.).

This painted tile from a tomb at Luoyang shows two scholars having a conversation (50 B.C.-A.D. 50).

A master teaches his pupils who sit in a typical revering posture.

These books contain the heart of the knowledge of ancient China. In them is found the ideal of a social class of which Confucius and his learned followers were the representatives. This ideal was based on a rule called the Five Relationships. The rule said that the common good took precedence over the individual's good. The rule applied to all the classes. According to this rule, the community is divided into four classes: enlightened people, farmers, artisans, and merchants. The learned people were models for the other classes.

In Confucianism, humanity is the highest virtue. A ruler must be able to rule the country with a global perspective on daily problems and follow the right principles established in ancient times. These principles were followed in the golden age, previous to the decline of kings and administrators devoid of virtue. Confucius and all the thinkers of his school believed in the utility of teaching and in the possibility of progress for humankind and society.

Two Branches of Confucian Thought

The philosopher Mencius (Meng tzu) (390-305 B.C.) is the first to have written down Confucius's teachings. Mencius's thoughts had an important impact upon Chinese society. Especially important was his belief that human nature is basically good.

Some decades later, Xunzi (315-236 B.C.) offered a new interpretation. Xunzi believed human nature to be evil. Because of this evil nature, Xunzi felt, people will not do anything if they are not forced to. Despite this, he believed that society could be bettered but only through education and moral guidance. He emphasized the importance of these elements in social order.

From Xunzi's thoughts, the so-called Legalist doctrine was born. Legalism, which stressed the importance of authority and strict laws, was first put into practice during the Qin dynasty. The doctrine was effective. The Qin dynasty expanded its control throughout China and created a centralized empire.

Daoism

The Daoist religion arose along with this Confucian line of thought, which focused on the human being within an organized society. Daoism encouraged people to search for a way to live according to the laws of the universe and not only with human laws. The word *dao,* in fact, originally meant "road" or "way." The oldest Daoist text is the *Classic of the Way and the Virtue (Daodejing).* It is believed to have been written by Lao-tzu. According to legend, Lao-tzu was a wise man who lived over five centuries before Christ.

The achievements of Chinese thought between the end of the Warring States period and the beginning of the Han Empire are now well known. Due to archaeological work, texts from before the rising of the empire have been found. These texts show a variety of original traditions. The excavations of Mawangdui have discovered works such as medical manuscripts and writings on astronomy. The excavations of Linyi have revealed important works on military strategy.

Above and below: These graphics were taken from Neolithic ceramics of the Yangshao culture.

The Writing

Chinese writing bears no relationship with the spoken language. The signs 1 and 2, for example, can be read and pronounced in different ways for every spoken language in the world. This is true of any element of Chinese writing, except for a few grammatical or specific signs. Signs whose interpretation is uncertain appear on Neolithic ceramics. Perhaps they were a kind of coded writing. Chinese writing was born and developed during the Bronze Age as a means for preserving the questions and answers from divination rituals.

During the Zhou period, writing became more refined, orderly, and widespread. The beautiful carved or cast inscriptions on bronze vases are the main evidence of this evolution. The ancient inscriptions were written in a "seal" style. This means that they were still similar to the writing on seals and personal stamps and thus varied widely from region to region.

With the foundation of the empire in 221 B.C., a new form of writing was developed from the ancient form. The unified administrative writing, or lishu, would become the writing of the Han emperors, and between A.D. 400 and 600 it would evolve into the decoded style. This style is considered the "model" of elegant Chinese writing. Today it is still the favorite form of writing. Among the writing materials being used at this time were the bamboo rolls. They were made of narrow bamboo strips, tied together by little strings.

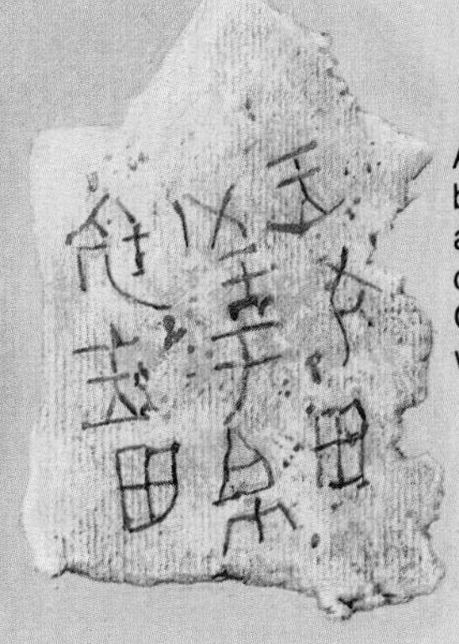

An oracle bone shows an example of early Chinese writing.

Some writing was set in metal.

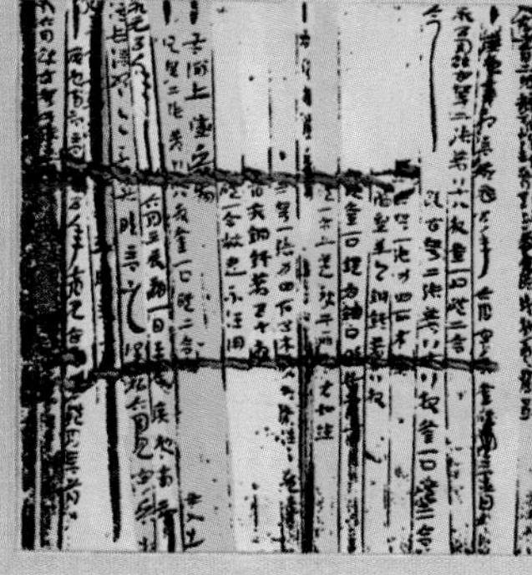

Early texts are shown written on narrow bamboo strips.

These documents were written in lishu, a more refined form of writing developed around 200 B.C.

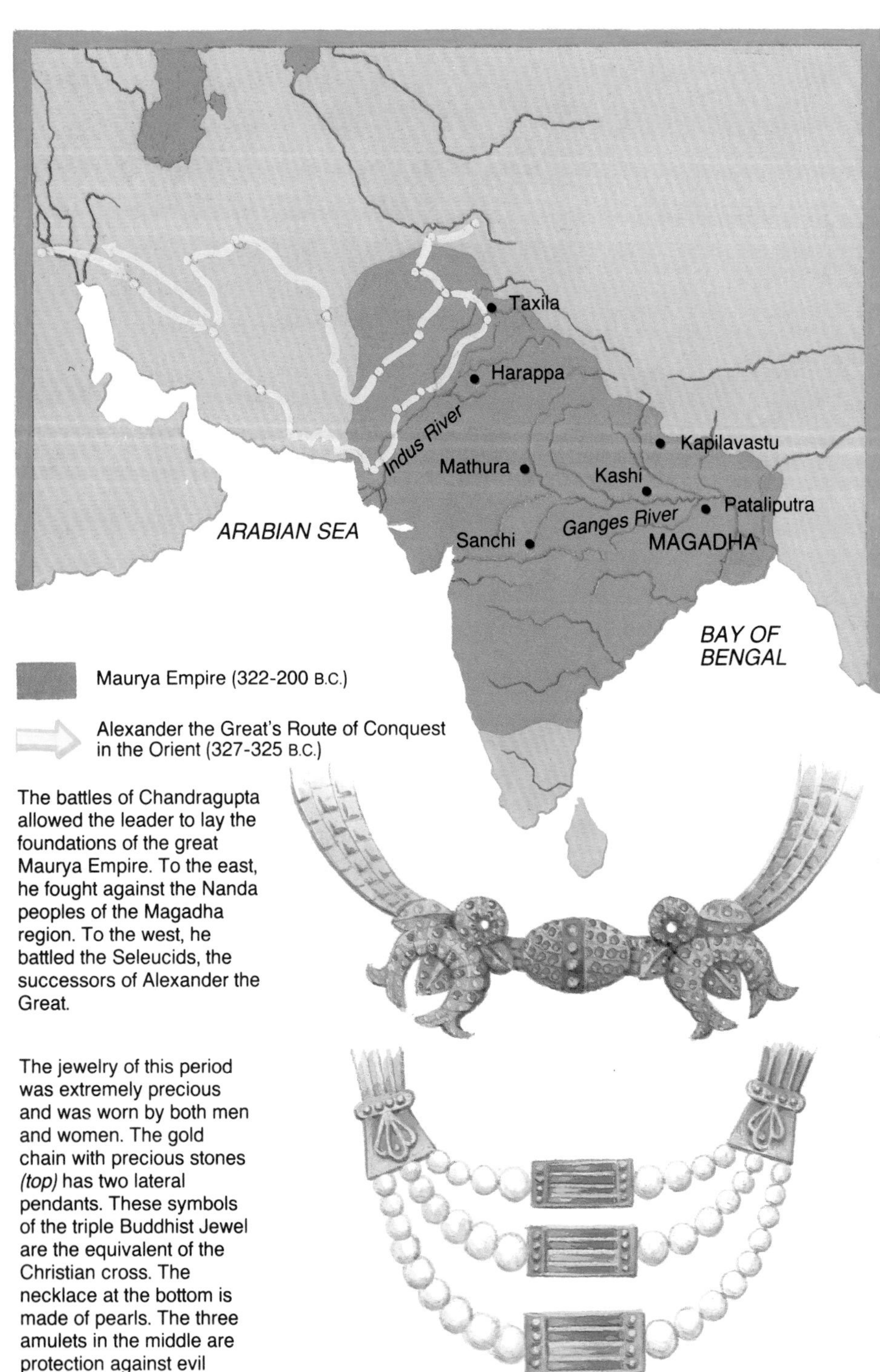

The battles of Chandragupta allowed the leader to lay the foundations of the great Maurya Empire. To the east, he fought against the Nanda peoples of the Magadha region. To the west, he battled the Seleucids, the successors of Alexander the Great.

The jewelry of this period was extremely precious and was worn by both men and women. The gold chain with precious stones *(top)* has two lateral pendants. These symbols of the triple Buddhist Jewel are the equivalent of the Christian cross. The necklace at the bottom is made of pearls. The three amulets in the middle are protection against evil forces.

This illustration shows life in a village during the Maurya Empire. This is a time of wealth, thanks to the vastness of the empire, which stretched from the Indus to the Ganges. Trading relationships with neighboring countries to the east and to the west also added to the wealth. The main cultivated crops were rice, wheat, millet, and sugar cane. In the background is a stupa, one of the most impressive architectural expressions of ancient India. Stupas were mound-shaped monuments. The dome was built with raw bricks and covered with fired bricks. Stupas contained relics of the Buddha or were built over sacred places where the Buddha had been. The most ancient stupas date back to the third century B.C.

THE MAURYA EMPIRE

India Enters History

With the foundation of the Maurya Empire in the third century B.C., it can be said that India entered history. Knowledge of its historical and human events no longer comes through fascinating legends. From this point on, it comes through precise documentation from archaeological finds, decoded epigraphs, and journals written by foreign travelers.

Chandragupta, the Founder

Between 500-400 B.C., the entire region of the Indus River came to be considered a separate province of the Persian Empire and was given the name of India. Around 330 B.C. when Alexander the Great defeated the Persian armies, the Indian territories became part of the dominion of this Macedonian leader. Alexander and his army reached the regions which today form the nation of Pakistan and the northwestern part of the Indian union.

When Alexander turned around and headed west again, Chandragupta (who belonged to an ancient clan known since the Buddha's time by the name of Maurya) took advantage of the moment's confusion and put himself at the head of a liberation movement. He fought and conquered the Macedonic garrisons which ruled over the former Persian provinces. After freeing the western territories from foreign rule, Chandragupta turned to the east and waged war against the Indian Nada dynasty, which ruled over the Magadha region. Then the Maurya leader stormed Pataliputra, the realm's capital (in 313 or 322 B.C.). In doing this, he founded the Maurya Empire, proclaiming himself its emperor.

Soon almost all of western India (except for the Himalaya regions and the southernmost areas) was part of Chandragupta's empire. His conquests may be considered the first true attempt at uniting the Indian subcontinent. Chandragupta organized his empire on a very solid uniform government. The structure he created ruled almost unchanged in all of the

This sculpture is from a column of the Stupa of Sanchi.

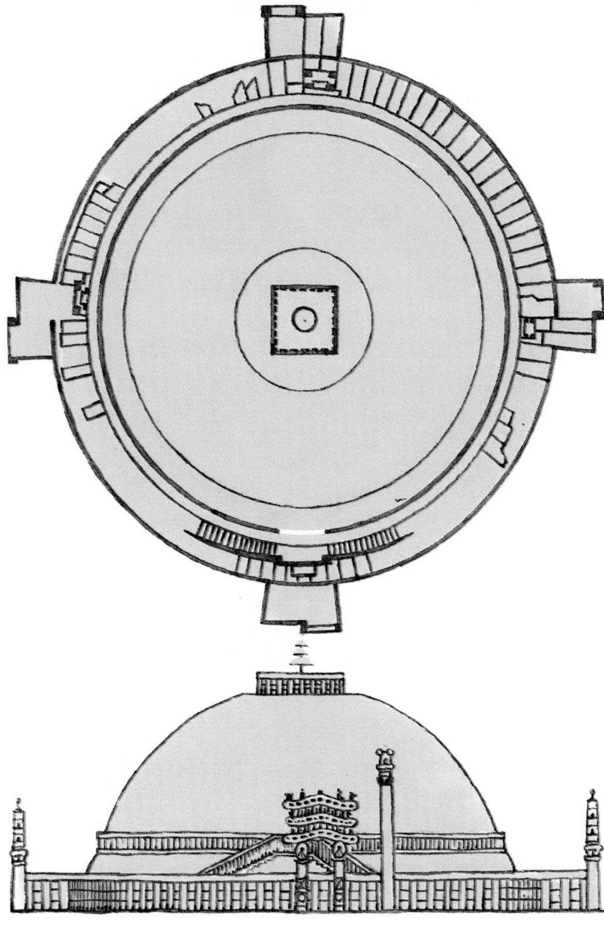

This print shows the plan and elevation of the Stupa of Sanchi, one of the famous stupas of the Maurya Empire. The central body of the building was built in the third century B.C. by Emperor Asoka.

following Indian empires. Chandragupta died in 297 B.C.. One of his many children, Bindusara, was his successor. Bindusara carried on his father's politics and pushed to the south in the attempt to expand the territories of the empire.

The *Arthashastra* and the Social Divisions

The main source of information on the Maurya Empire is the *Arthashastra.* This treatise on the art of good ruling was written by Chandragupta's famous minister, Kautilya. This text, which has reached the present time intact, describes the political and social organization of ancient India. The *Arthashastra* speaks of a "constitutional" monarchy in which the king headed the administration and also had all the power: military, legislative, and judicial.

The organization of the state was in the hands of a Council of the Ministers. The council was supported by two assemblies: the "City Council" and the "Kingdom Council." The king had to consult with both assemblies before he could place his seal on laws or proposals. Within this structure, great importance was placed on the Council of the Ministers, which had eighteen principal members.

Culture, Religion, and Art

The Maurya Empire marks one of the most prestigious moments of Indian cultural life. Some of the major literary works of India were written between 400 and 100 B.C. During this period, the most ancient parts of the epic poems *Ramayana* and *Mahabharata* were composed, and Patanjali wrote his basic text on yoga, the *Yoga Sutra,* and important texts on grammar. Moreover, the juducial-social manuals that illustrate the rights and duties of the various castes were being drawn up. The most widely practiced religion was Brahmanism in all its different forms, but Jainism and Buddhism were also present. As a result of the use of wood in architecture, monuments and buildings did not endure the passing of the centuries, and very little is left of the art of those times. The only artistic treasures which have been preserved are the mural paintings of Ajanta in central India, and some stupas, the typical funerary mounds of the Buddhist tradition.

ASOKA AND THE SPREAD OF BUDDHISM

Asoka: The Height of the Maurya Empire

The Maurya Empire reached its height under Asoka, the son of Bindusara and grandson of Chandragupta. Asoka took the throne in about 272 B.C. While still a boy, Asoka was elected viceroy for the regions of Ujjain and Taxila. By the time he became emperor, he already had some ruling experience. Asoka, who was known to be fierce and violent, followed his grandfather's policy of expansion. He at once started adding more territories to the empire.

An important event in Asoka's life was the Kalinga rebellion. Kalinga was the capital of an important realm on the eastern coast of India, south of today's Bengal. Asoka's fight against the Kalinga army was unbelievably cruel, even for those times. The realm of Kalinga suffered over 100,000 casualties, both of soldiers and civilians. In addition, more than 200,000 men and women were deported. But this tremendous slaughter later filled the emperor with remorse. In a deep religious crisis, he converted to Buddhism.

The Conversion to Buddhism

According to Buddhist sources, Asoka was converted by the monk Upagupta. Buddhism completely changed this monarch's cruel nature. Inspired and guided by the principles of the Buddha, Asoka became the most open-minded, tolerant ruler in Indian history. His reign is still remembered today as an example of mutual respect among the various religious and social factions existing in India at the time. Asoka tirelessly spread Buddhist religion both within his empire and abroad where he sent many missionary groups. He helped monasteries, communities, and Buddhist schools, but he was also very generous toward the Hindu and Jainist religions.

Under Asoka, Buddhism had its moment of greatest popularity in India. Practically all classes of Indian people were drawn toward this religion, which became the most widespread religion in the empire for a few centuries. Asoka, although respectful of other religions, made Buddhism the state religion and favored its spread throughout the empire's territories.

Cultural Achievements

Under Asoka, Indian art and culture of all types developed as never before. The emperor also greatly improved the social conditions of his people. He built hospitals, created irrigation systems for villages and fields, and established centers for the production of herbal medicines. He also ordered that the underground temples of Barabar be built and later donated them to the Hindu hermits of the Shiva school.

During the fifteenth year of his reign, Asoka enlarged the stupa which was raised near Kapilavastu and built many new ones. Moreover, Asoka is credited with the creation of Indian epigraphy, or the study of writing cut into material such as metal or stone. His public proclamations were often carved on tall stone columns, many of which are still intact today. These columns were erected in different locations throughout the territories of the empire. Most of these inscriptions were a type of moral propaganda. Through them, scholars have been able to retrace most of the history of the Maurya Empire, including important dates and events.

The Empire Under the Rule of Asoka

Asoka reigned over the largest empire ever known in ancient India. Pataliputra (today called Patna) was its capital. The realm's territories stretched to the west all the way to present-day Afghanistan; to the east they reached what is today Bengal. The entire south-central part of India was under Asoka's dominion, with the only exceptions being the southern realms of Chola, Pandya, Chera, and Satyaputra, which were independent. When Asoka died in 232 B.C., the empire was immediately divided among his numerous sons. Within a few decades, this fragmentation would cause the end of the Maurya Empire. Brihadratha, the last Maurya monarch, was killed by one of his generals. With him, the golden period of Indian history ended, and a long period of political division and military tension began.

Characters and customs of the Maurya society are depicted. **1)** This subject has given a sum of money for the construction of a stupa. He wears a mauli, the typical Indian turban tied at the forehead. **2)** A woman wears the very common cotton veil, called an uttarya, over her head. Necklaces and bracelets decorate her neck, wrists, and ankles. **3)** A warrior wears one of the early types of tunics, tailored and sewn. Over his shoulder, he carries his sheathed sword. **4)** A court woman wears the antarya. This white cotton or linen cloth was used by both men and women. It was held around the hips with belts and wrapped between the legs. **5)** This noblewoman's turban is decorated with a heart-shaped pin. **6)** A head maid displays a peculiar, saddle-shaped hairstyle. Many of these reconstructions are based on sculptures of the Maurya epoch.

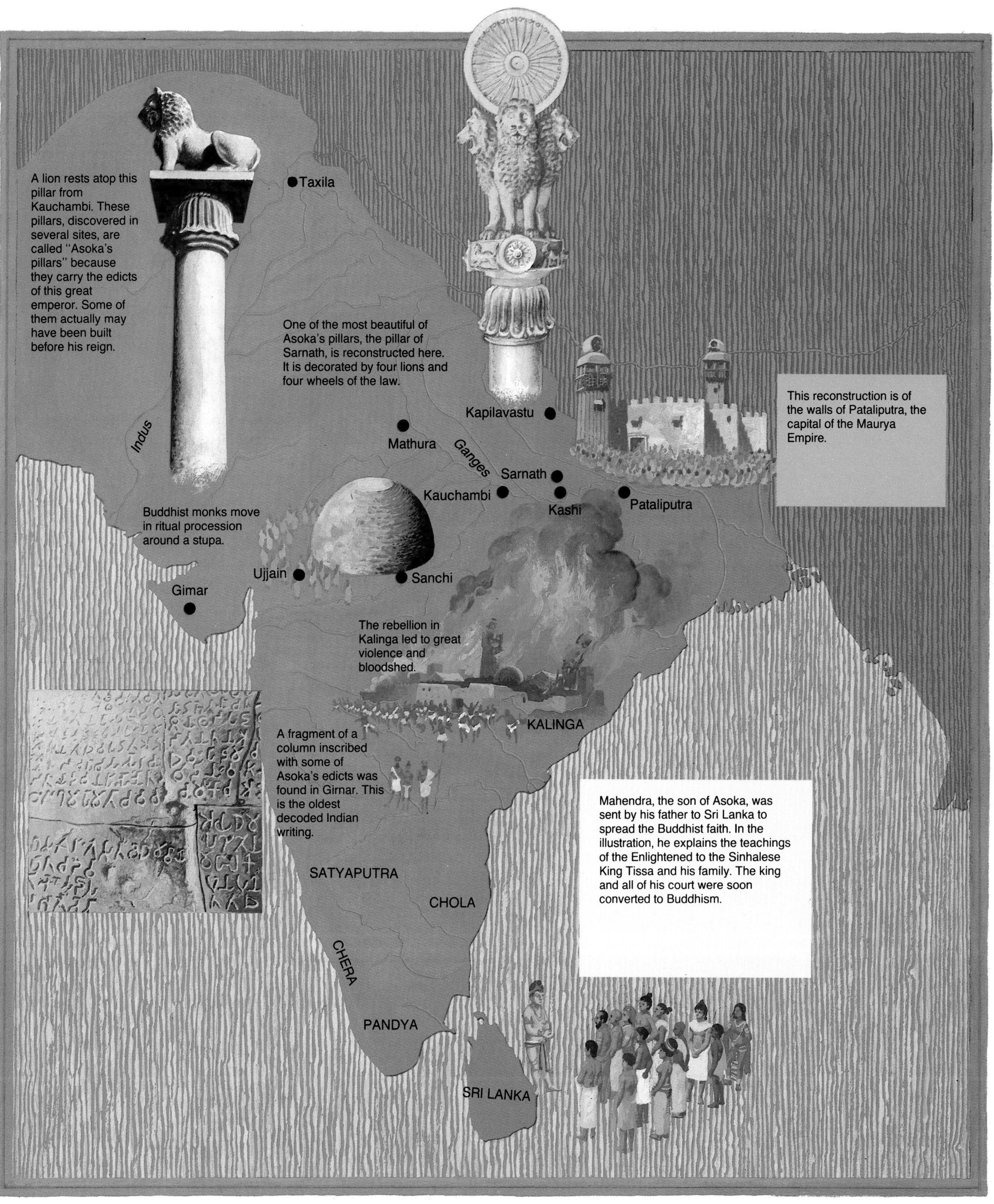

A lion rests atop this pillar from Kauchambi. These pillars, discovered in several sites, are called "Asoka's pillars" because they carry the edicts of this great emperor. Some of them actually may have been built before his reign.

One of the most beautiful of Asoka's pillars, the pillar of Sarnath, is reconstructed here. It is decorated by four lions and four wheels of the law.

This reconstruction is of the walls of Pataliputra, the capital of the Maurya Empire.

Buddhist monks move in ritual procession around a stupa.

The rebellion in Kalinga led to great violence and bloodshed.

A fragment of a column inscribed with some of Asoka's edicts was found in Girnar. This is the oldest decoded Indian writing.

Mahendra, the son of Asoka, was sent by his father to Sri Lanka to spread the Buddhist faith. In the illustration, he explains the teachings of the Enlightened to the Sinhalese King Tissa and his family. The king and all of his court were soon converted to Buddhism.

THE SATAVAHANA EMPIRE AND THE SOUTHERN KINGDOMS

After the fall of the Maurya Empire (185 B.C.), the states of north-central and eastern India went through a long period of political and military fragmentation. Apart from a notable group of small local realms, the Shunga dynasty, together with the Kanva dynasty, asserted itself for about a year. (Pushyamitra, who founded the Shunga dynasty, killed Brihadratha, the last Maurya ruler.) These two dynasties did not leave any special mark in Indian history. More interesting was the Satavahana dynasty which ruled over south-central India (with the exception of the southernmost states) between 50 B.C. and A.D. 250.

The first Satavahana king was Simuka. After destroying the last traces of the Shunga and Kanva governments, Simuka founded his dynasty in 30 B.C. He kept the throne for twenty-three years. Simuka was followed by his brother Krishna, who conquered more territories and reigned for eighteen years. When Krishna died, the Satavahana Empire covered almost all of south-central India, and the monarchs had taken on the name of "Lords of the Southern Lands."

The following king in this dynasty was Satakarni, the son or grandson (according to different sources) of Simuka. Satakarni further extended his territories through various wars. Satakarni the Second succeeded Satakarni and was the first in a long series of kings who would consolidate the Satavahana Empire. Among them, the only one of any importance was the seventh in the dynasty, Hala, who conquered Sri Lanka around A.D. 78.

The twenty-third Satavahana emperor was Gautamiputra Satakarni, who reigned in the first decades of the second century A.D. This ruler came into power during a period of decline in his dynasty. At the time, his realm was limited to the central region, and the situation threatened to get even worse. But with a series of successful battles, Gautamiputra Satakarni again expanded his empire's territory, annexing most of today's state of Gujarat. Gautamiputra gave himself the title of "the monarch whose subjects drink from the waters of three oceans." This meant that the Satavahana territories stretched from the Arabian Sea to the Indian Ocean to the Bay of Bengal. During the second century A.D., Gautamiputra's son, Vasishtiputra Pulumayi, succeeded him to the throne. He lost some western regions but conquered more land to the southeast. The successors of Pulumayi were Shivashri Satakarni (A.D. 159-166), Shivaskanda Satakarni (A.D. 167-174), and Yajnashri Satakarni, the last great Satavahana king (A.D. 175-203). After Yajnashri Satakarni, the empire broke into many small independent princedoms.

The Kingdoms of the Far South

The far south of India was inhabited by Tamil populations who were unaffected by the Indo-European invasions. This region was also left untouched by the expansion of the Satavahana Empire. The southernmost territories of India were divided into the kingdoms of Chola, Pandya, and Chera. The Chola and Pandya dynasties ruled respectively on the northern and southern regions of today's state of Tamil-Nadu. The Chera ruled on the land which today forms the state of Kerala. Even Asoka had not successfully conquered these southern realms.

Sri Lanka

Since ancient times, the history of Sri Lanka has been intimately connected to that of India. Evidence of these first relationships is the Hindu epic poem *Ramayana,* where the island of Sri Lanka is mentioned as the residence of the demon Ravana. Ravana had abducted Sita, the companion of the poem's hero, Rama.

Around 500 B.C., an army coming from northern India invaded Sri Lanka. It was led by a monarch called Vijaya. These Aryan invaders came from the sea and had probably started from a harbor located in the region of the Gulf of Cambay. At that time, Sri Lanka was inhabited by primitive peoples, whose origin is still unknown.

The invaders brought an Indo-Aryan language to the island (the Sinhalese language), as well as the Hindu religion, and even a caste system. They mainly colonized the coast and some valleys, pushing the local tribes into remote inland regions. Hinduism and the related Brahmanic rituals soon spread throughout the island. The caste system underwent some modifications in the island. As a result, the society was more or less divided into two main classes called kulina and hina. The nobles, warriors, and landowners belonged to the first class. The second class was divided into several professional subclasses, some of which had important tasks in the society. At the bottom end of the scale were the dasa, who were the slaves. Here, as in India, the slaves were used almost exclusively for housework.

The arrival of a committee of Buddhist missionaries was an important event in the history of Sri Lanka. The missionaries, sent by the Emperor Asoka and led by his son Mahendra, soon converted King Tissa and all of his court to Buddhism. In a very short time, most of the population of the island had also converted.

The Sinhalese art was greatly influenced by the spread of Buddhism. In fact, the Buddhist spirit inspired most of the artistic creations in Sri Lanka. Among the most important works of art are the impressive Stupas of Anuradhapura in the northern part of the island, the Buddha of Polannarukeil (a huge statue carved into a rock wall, depicting the Buddha in the act of reaching nirvana) in the central regions, and the frescoes of Sigiriya, also in the central part of the island, which have style and contents that are similar to the Indian paintings of Ajanta.

At the beginning of the Christian era, the Dravidic populations from southern India began to invade Sri Lanka. The new invaders settled mainly in the northern part of the island. These invasions resulted in the penetrating influence of the Tamil culture and language on the island. Even today, the ethnic Tamil minority of Sri Lanka numbers a few million people.

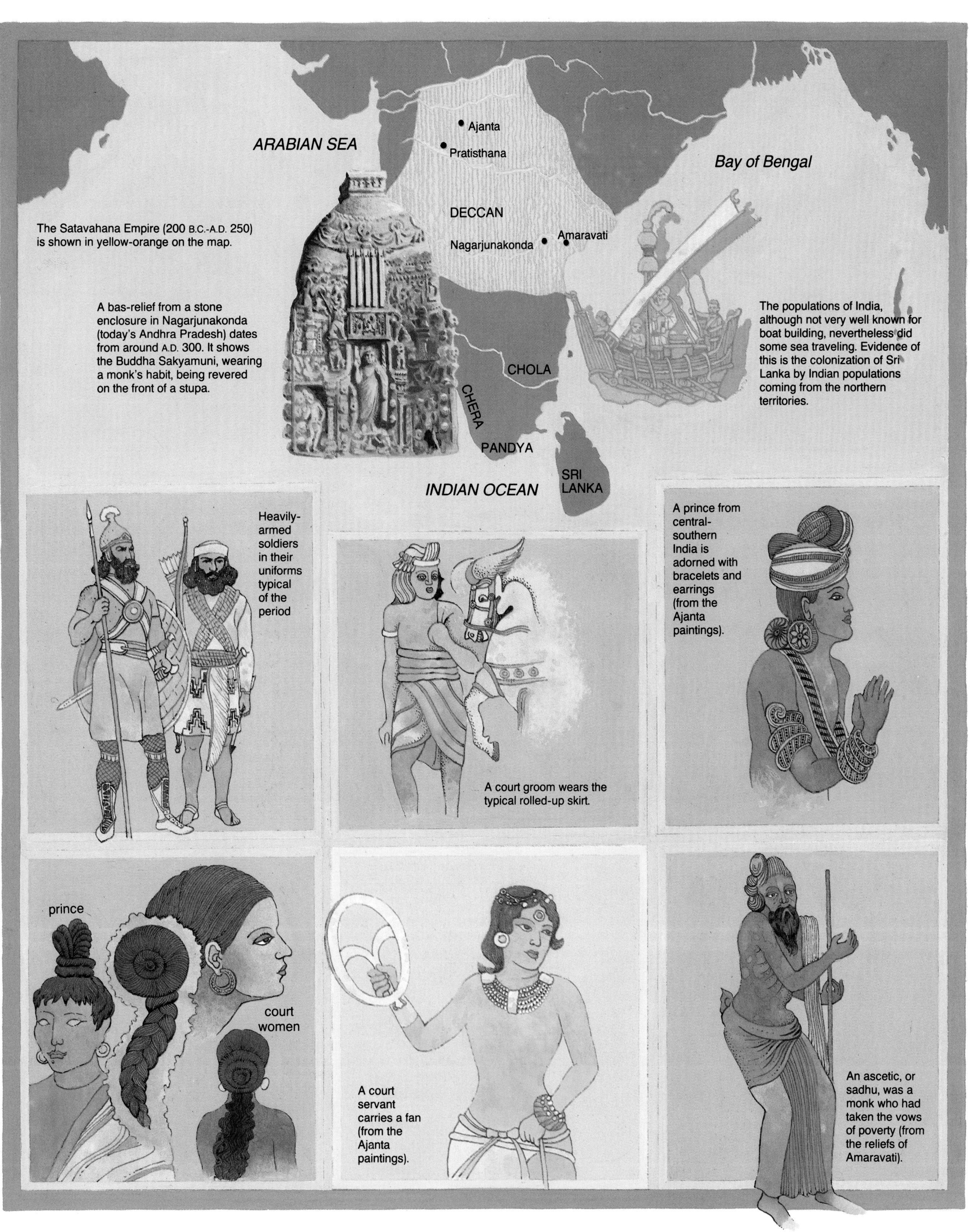

The Satavahana Empire (200 B.C.-A.D. 250) is shown in yellow-orange on the map.

A bas-relief from a stone enclosure in Nagarjunakonda (today's Andhra Pradesh) dates from around A.D. 300. It shows the Buddha Sakyamuni, wearing a monk's habit, being revered on the front of a stupa.

The populations of India, although not very well known for boat building, nevertheless did some sea traveling. Evidence of this is the colonization of Sri Lanka by Indian populations coming from the northern territories.

Heavily-armed soldiers in their uniforms typical of the period

A court groom wears the typical rolled-up skirt.

A prince from central-southern India is adorned with bracelets and earrings (from the Ajanta paintings).

A court servant carries a fan (from the Ajanta paintings).

An ascetic, or sadhu, was a monk who had taken the vows of poverty (from the reliefs of Amaravati).

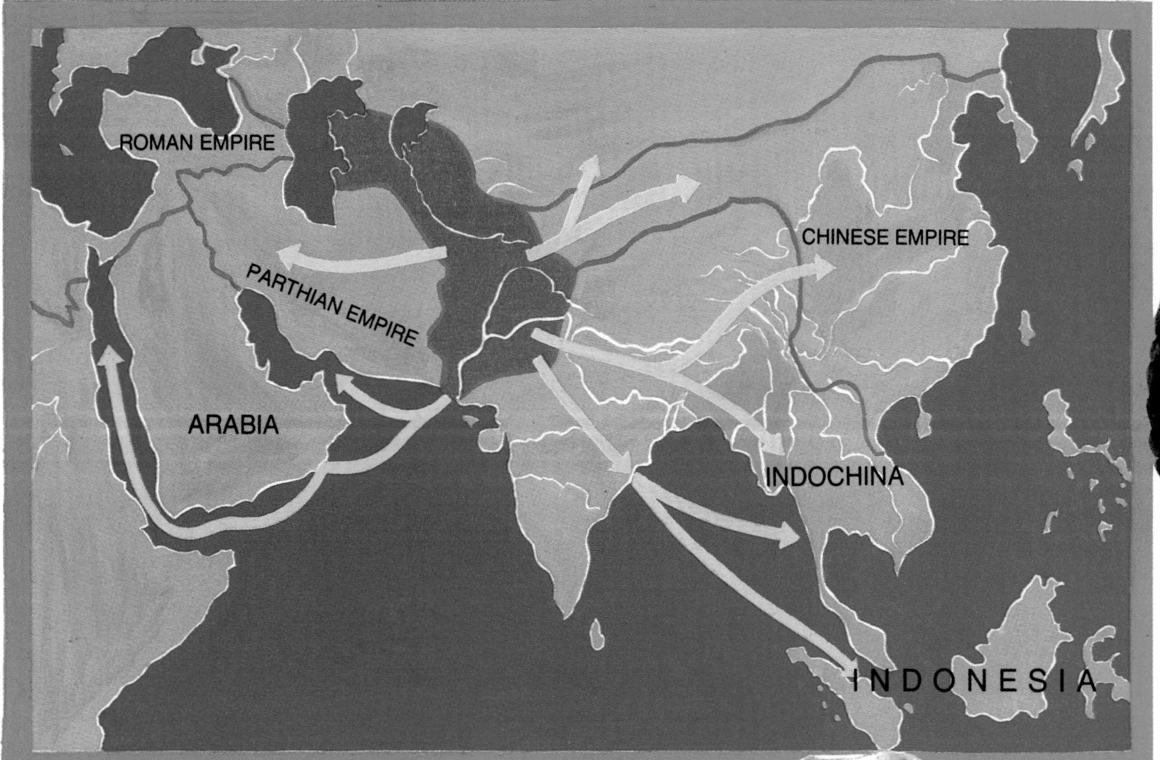

The map shows the trading relationships established by the Kushan Empire *(in red)*, both with the Greek-Roman world to the west and with the Chinese Empire and southeastern Asia to the east. This was one of the most intense periods of trade development in Indian history.

This statue of Buddha, from the fifth century A.D., is an example of Guptan art with Mathura influence.

This statue of King Kanishka was probably originally kept inside the family temple of the Kushan kings in Mathura. The monarch is dressed in the middle eastern fashion of the Parthians, with a tunic, pants, a long cloak, and lined boots. He is holding two swords. His head is missing as a result of vandalism by the Muslims. These invaders conquered the city as well as all the territories of central-northern India about 2000 B.C.

THE KUSHAN PERIOD

After the fall of the Maurya Empire (185 B.C.), the situation in India was rather confusing. On the Ganges plain there was a group of small but independent realms with various populations fighting and attempting to push into the country along the northern borders. Among these peoples were the Scythians who played a relatively important role in Indian history. They were a group of minor Iranian tribes who had come from the north. At first they pushed into western Afghanistan, but the Parthian, Macedonian, and Indo-Hellenic armies kept them temporarily at bay. When the power of these realms decreased, the Scythians crossed the border into Afghanistan. From there, they reached the Indus valley and conquered all of the territories which today form the states of Pakistan and Punjab. In 80 B.C., they stormed Taxila, then split up into several small monarchies scattered throughout northwestern India. Soon the Scythians mingled with the local populations, embraced the Indian religions, and were no longer a separate ethnic entity.

The Arrival of the Kushans

Around 126 B.C., a population of Chinese origin called Yueh-Chi invaded the Battriana region (northeastern Iran) and settled there. In A.D. 48 one of the tribes of the Yueh-Chi, called Kushan, occupied the Indian region of Gandhara (along the course of the Indus River, the stretch of territory between today's towns of Peshawar and Rawalpindi), chasing away the last Indo-Hellenic king, Ermeo. Under the guidance of an energetic and enterprising monarch, Kadphises I, the Kushans conquered Taxila and most of the Kashmir valley, founding a new empire which stretched from the western borders of Afghanistan to today's Punjab. Kadphises II further increased the extent of his realm by annexing many regions of northwestern India, including the city of Mathura.

King Kanishka

Undoubtedly, the greatest of all the Kushan kings was Kanishka. He completely conquered the Indian regions of the northwest, established his capital at Purushapura (today called Peshawar), and invaded central India. He even attacked the Chinese Empire, forcing it to surrender the provinces of Kashgar, Yarkand, and

Gandhara art from the third century A.D. shows Bodhisattva Maytreya carved on dark stone.

Gandhara art from A.D. 200-300, shows Buddha in the lotus position.

Kushan warriors, led by their commander riding in a war chariot, attack and defeat a Parthian army. Since very ancient times, the Indians used specially trained elephants in battle.

A Greek artist working at the Kushana court carves a statue in the presence of the king and two of his guards. Gandhara art was heavily influenced by Greek art. This influence is proof of the cultural exchanges between India and the western world during the first centuries A.D.

Khotan. Thus, Kanishka ruled over an empire which stretched from south-central Asia to the Ganges plain and included the Indus valley, Afghanistan, Kashmir, and the Pamir region.

Not much is known about Kanishka's administration. But from the little information that is available, it seems likely that he ruled his empire by an efficient feudal system. Satraps, or governors, were the connecting link between the provinces and the central power, and the subjects lived in prosperity. During his reign, Kanishka converted to Buddhism. He later ordered the construction of numerous stupas and monasteries. Although he was a Buddhist, Kanishka was tolerant of other religions in his empire.

Kanishka's successor was Vanishka (A.D. 168-172), after whom Atuvishka took the throne. Atuvishka seems to have reigned for a long time over a prosperous and peaceful empire. The last great sovereign of the dynasty was Vasudeva I. He ruled from about A.D. 218-242 and was probably Atuvishka's successor. After Vasudeva I, however, the empire experienced a rapid decline, and the entire structure collapsed within a few decades.

Kushan Art: Gandhara and Mathura

The Kushan period is characterized by intense artistic activity. Two schools were born in this period, that of Gandhara and that of Mathura. Both took their names from the localities where they developed. Gandhara art, also called Indo-Hellenic or Greek-Buddhist, applied Greek style to Indian subjects, especially those of Buddhist tradition. This school's works of art have a lot in common with the statues of the Greek and Roman world, and the bodhisattva of Gandhara look much like images of Apollo.

The Mathura art, on the other hand, is truly Indian. It is the expression of one of the most intense and meaningful moments of artistic creativity in India. Especially characteristic are the images of Buddha Sakyamuni, shown seated in the meditation posture. This is the image of the Buddha which will be used as a prototype throughout all of Buddhist Indian art.

Seen here is the Trimurti of the Hindu pantheon. Brahma is the Creator; Vishnu is the Preserver; and Shiva is the Destroyer.

In a scene from the *Mahabharata,* the god Krishna rides the chariot of the warrior Arjuna and teaches him the duties of the perfect Hindu follower.

The *Mahabharata*

The *Mahabharata* is one of the two great poems of the Indian tradition. It is a wide collection, both of narrative and educational literature, which includes myths, popular traditions, and legends about the main Hindu deities. All of this material, with the passage of time, took the form of an epic poem which describes the extended battle between two families over the control of north-central India. This region is called Bharata in epic poetry, and the title of the poem refers to this name.

The date of composition of the work and the names of its authors have not yet been determined with accuracy. However, it seems likely that a version more or less similar to the present one was written in the second century A.D. The text of the *Mahabharata* is a useful source of information on habits and customs of ancient India.

THE HINDU RELIGION

The Puranic Period

About the beginning of the second century B.C., the rapid growth of both Buddhism and Jainism threw the world of Vedic doctrine into crisis. Its rigid structure, centered on the Brahman (the priest), no longer met the needs of the times. Thus inside the Brahmanic tradition, new ideas began to grow.

The ancient Hindu gods started to play les important roles, and new deities took their pla ces. Especially important was the Trimurt (trinity) of Brahma, Vishnu, and Shiva. All o these changes took place without an officia break from the religion. In fact, they seemed t(come from within it. Some of the new gods such as Shiva, had been absent from the Hindı pantheon before this period. But others, such a: Vishnu, had been part of the ancient group oi gods but had been of secondary importance These new gods gained importance through slow but constant pressure from a culture that the Aryans had conquered during their invasion of India. This culture, its ideas, and sometimes actual populations continued to push their way into the Indo-European world. They somehow took revenge on the conquerors by slipping at least part of their culture into the Vedic world.

The liturgy itself was influenced by the change. References to the Veda's authority became less frequent around the beginning of the Christian age. A new collection of texts, called *Purana,* gained importance. The word *Purana* means "collections of the stories of the ancient times." From the Brahmanic point of view, the *Purana* were an extension of the Veda. They were a more simple means of spreading religious teachings to larger numbers of people. Actually, the meeting of the Indo-European

A night with a full moon was considered especially favorable for sacred ceremonies. In this drawing, a procession of women goes to the forest temple on such a night. In front of the temple sits the Brahman, who is the temple's keeper and is in charge of conducting the rituals. Also in the picture, two priests meditate in front of their cave dwellings. Past the forest, a typical Indian village is situated on the riverbank.

In a scene from the *Ramayana,* Rama and Sita sit in adoration before a symbol of the union of the male and female entities.

traditions with the religious cultures of pre-Aryan India is attained in and with the *Purana.* From them, the feminine elements gained a new importance in the Hindu pantheon. Each male deity was given a female counterpart, and brand new cults of female deities developed. The cult of trees and water also spread.

The Hindu Pantheon

In the new dimension of Hindu religion, importance is given to the Trimurti of Brahma, Shiva, and Vishnu. In short, the idea of divinity can be seen through the basic forms of these three deities: Creator (Brahma), Preserver (Vishnu), and Destroyer (Shiva). Each main deity has his own family, generally including a female counterpart (shakti, in the Sanscrit language), a particular animal which is considered that god's "vehicle of expression," and other minor deities.

Drawing, top of page: Durga is one of the main female gods of the Hindu pantheon. She has an infinite number of arms and brandishes a symbolic object in each hand. Kali is the terrifying goddess with a dark complexion and four arms. In her hands she holds the cut off heads of the enemies of the gods, a curved knife, a bowl of blood, and a club. Around her neck she wears a necklace of skulls, and her skirt is made of arms. This deity symbolizes dynamic power carried all the way to destruction.

The *Ramayana*

The *Ramayana* is the other great epic poem of classic India. It is composed of seven books and narrates the adventures and the heroic deeds of Rama and of his companion, Sita. Originally, it was thought that the poet Valmiki wrote the *Ramayana.* Today, however, it seems certain that the text went through several stages of development and was subject to several additions and revisions. Also, as with the *Mahabharata,* dating the *Ramayana,* is not an easy task. Most likely, it is older than the *Mahabharata.* According to most sources, the core of the *Ramayana* was composed from 500-300 B.C. Various additions were made between 300 B.C. and A.D. 200. The adventures narrated in the *Ramayana* are very popular even in modern day India, and they are often the subject of religious plays.

THE GUPTAN EMPIRE

The Guptan Emperors

The Guptan period is considered the golden age of Indian history and culture. The Gupta founded an empire which covered a great part of the Indian continent. This dynasty corresponded with great development in the arts, literature, and philosophical sciences. About A.D. 400, India went through a great period of political fragmentation. As a result, a large number of small states formed, particularly in the Ganges valley. These states were often in disagreement, and they sometimes warred with each other.

One of these kingdoms was called Maghada. It was ruled by Chandra Gupta, who was one of the most intelligent and politically insightful rulers that India had ever had. In a short time, Chandra Gupta (who reigned from A.D. 310 to 335) conquered most of the neighboring states and expanded his realm to include most of the territory of what is today Bihar and a large part of the lands toward the Bay of Bengal. In A.D. 320, he founded the Guptan Empire and declared the city of Pataliputra the capital. This empire would last nearly two hundred years.

His successor, Samudragupta (A.D. 335-375), carried on Chandra Gupta's unification work. With continuous and victorious battles, he conquered over thirty-five kingdoms from the Ganges to the Indus rivers from today's Punjab to the northern regions of Deccan. Like his father, Samudragupta was a brilliant military commander and statesman. Actually, some scholars consider him the true founder of the Guptan Empire.

Chandra Gupta II (A.D. 375-414) combined the victories of his predecessors and completed the unification of central-western India. This included conquering the Ujjayini, a royal family who ruled over a wide territory roughly located between the central Indian region and the Deccan plateau. The capital of this realm, Ujjain, was considered the main intellectual center of the time. After seizing it, Chandra Gupta II was so impressed with its charm that he decided to make it the capital of his empire.

Social and Economic Life

Under Kumara Gupta (414-455), the successor of Chandra Gupta II, the refined and elegant Guptan civilization reached its height. Indian society under this dynasty lived through a period of incredible prosperity, of religious and civil freedom, and of artistic, literary, and architectural blossoming. Moreover, the political structure itself was sound and effective. The throne was inherited but not necessarily by the firstborn. The council of the ministers did not have executive powers, but the monarch would listen to its advice. The division of power was well distributed at all levels. The villages, which were ruled by a leader, began again to take a major role in Indian society. The importance of the cities began to decline. Meanwhile, trade and cultural exchanges were greatly enhanced.

Near the end of Kumara Gupta's reign, the Huns, a warlike people from the Asian steppes, started to create pressure along the empire's borders. Skanda Gupta (455-467) succeeded in keeping the Huns at bay momentarily. After his death, the empire rapidly fell apart. No longer meeting any resistance, the Huns swarmed all over, reaching the Punjab region and some areas of the Rajputana region (today's Rajasthan). It was the end of the Guptan Empire.

Art, Religion, and Philosophy

During the Guptan period, Indian art underwent an exceptional period of blossoming. Some of the major artistic treasures of India belong to this period (such as the Caves of Ajanta). Art was still expressing Buddhist content, but it already reflected the return of Hinduism as the main religion in India. Actually, although Buddhist influence was still present in art, symptoms of its decline were already noticeable. At the same time, Hinduism was gaining strength. It began to establish itself all over the country as the "true" Indian religion. Also during this time, philosophy achieved its highest level with Samkya thought. This was perhaps the most profound and most modern of all Indian philosophies. It saw matter as a never-ending transformation of energy and showed insight into the relative nature of space. The Guptan period was also the golden epoch of Sanskrit literature, and the great poet Kalidasa (who probably lived at the time of Chandra Gupta II) was often invited to the Guptan court.

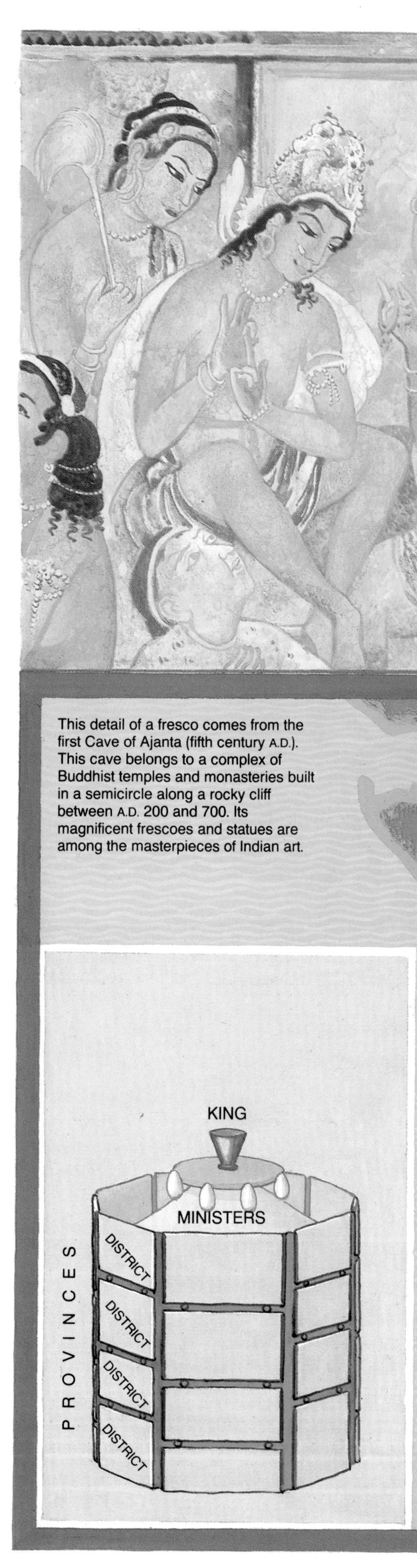

This detail of a fresco comes from the first Cave of Ajanta (fifth century A.D.). This cave belongs to a complex of Buddhist temples and monasteries built in a semicircle along a rocky cliff between A.D. 200 and 700. Its magnificent frescoes and statues are among the masterpieces of Indian art.

In plum, the map shows the Guptan Empire along the Ganges River and in the neighboring regions. The most important centers in political, artistic, and religious life are also indicated. *To the right, inset:* At the peak of the Guptan Empire was the king, who was advised by a counsel of ministers. The empire was divided into provinces ruled by governors. These governors, who usually belonged to the royal family, were appointed directly by the king. The provinces were, in turn, divided into districts. Within the districts, the vital unit of Guptan society was the village, with its own chief.

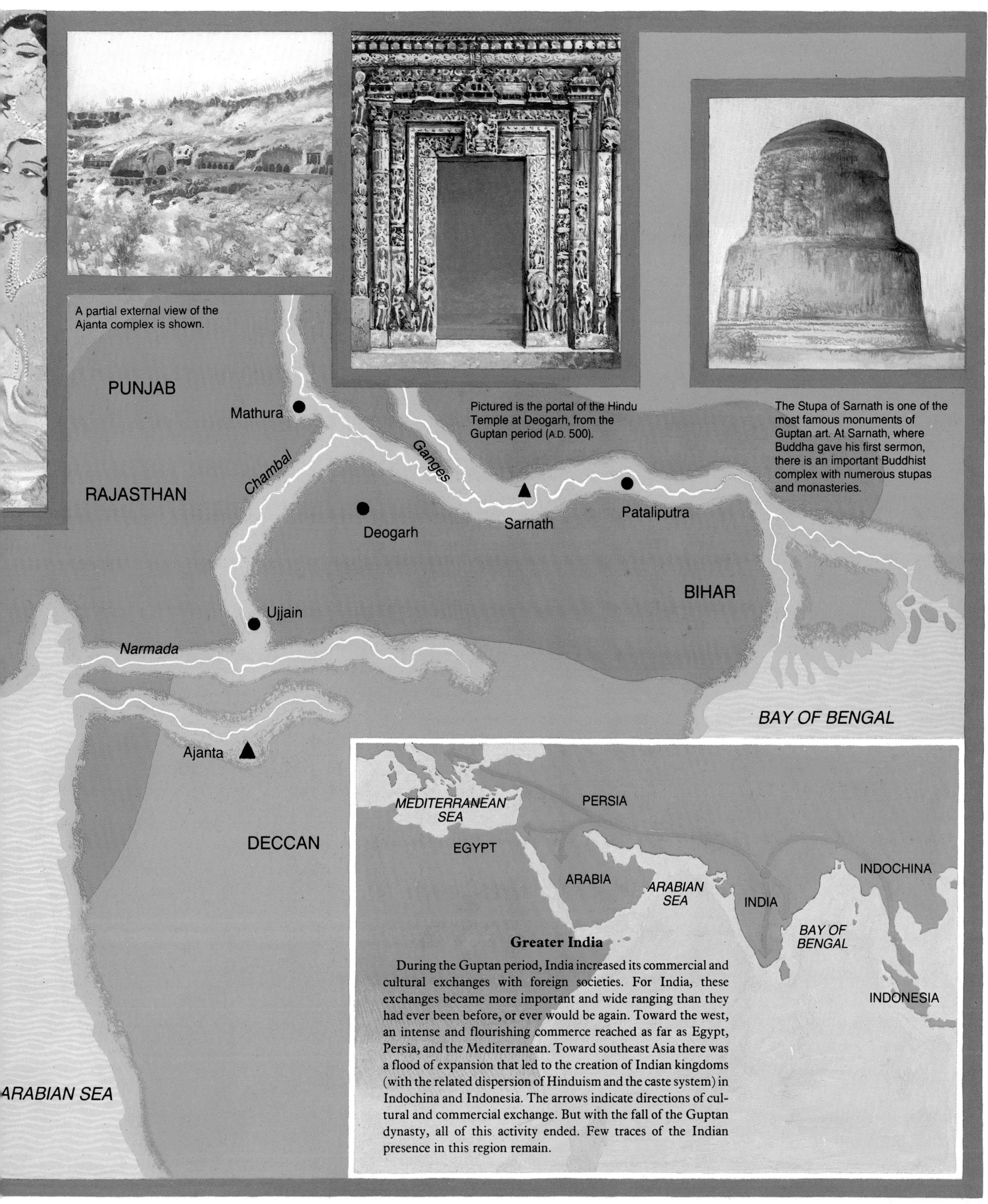

A partial external view of the Ajanta complex is shown.

Pictured is the portal of the Hindu Temple at Deogarh, from the Guptan period (A.D. 500).

The Stupa of Sarnath is one of the most famous monuments of Guptan art. At Sarnath, where Buddha gave his first sermon, there is an important Buddhist complex with numerous stupas and monasteries.

Greater India

During the Guptan period, India increased its commercial and cultural exchanges with foreign societies. For India, these exchanges became more important and wide ranging than they had ever been before, or ever would be again. Toward the west, an intense and flourishing commerce reached as far as Egypt, Persia, and the Mediterranean. Toward southeast Asia there was a flood of expansion that led to the creation of Indian kingdoms (with the related dispersion of Hinduism and the caste system) in Indochina and Indonesia. The arrows indicate directions of cultural and commercial exchange. But with the fall of the Guptan dynasty, all of this activity ended. Few traces of the Indian presence in this region remain.

This man and his son, dressed in rough leather clothing, belong to a nomadic Tibetan tribe.

Top left: The Tibetans called Guru Padmasambhava "the second Buddha" because of his great importance in the history of Tibetan Buddhism. He is the symbol of self-inspired energy, of the magical qualities of the highest forms of Buddhism, and of the final inner liberation. Padmasambhava was mainly responsible for the spread of Buddhism in Tibet.

The geographical position of Tibet is shown (in light blue) within central Asia. Its great strategic importance between China to the northeast and India to the south is clear.

TIBET

The First Kings

Tibet is known in the world for being, until the last decade or so, the most inaccessible Asian country. The origins of this nation are still, to a large degree, unknown. This is partly due to the fact that it is surrounded to the south, north, and west by some of the highest mountains in the world. It seems that the central element of the Tibetan population came from several nomadic tribes originating in north-central Asia.

From this rough and chaotic world of nomads and shepherds, a sort of feudal confederation began to form toward the end of the sixth century A.D. This group settled in the area along the right bank of the Brahmaputra River. Soon after, they conquered and unified almost all of the regions of central Tibet and pushed even farther, all the way to the Indian borders. As noted, this was not a rigidly centralized state. Rather, it was a feudal confederation in which the local princes had most of the power. The most important king of the dynasty was Song-Tsan Gam-Po. He reigned with insight and justice, favored many artistic and cultural projects, and gave the Tibetan people a written language.

According to the custom of the time, Tsan Gam-Po had two wives. One was from Nepal, and one was from China. They were both fervent Buddhists and, through their efforts, the first elements of Buddhism entered Tibet. The

This drawing captures a typical Tibetan landscape. In the background rise the high mountains, covered with snow even in the summer. At the foot of the mountains stretches a green plateau. In the distance, to the left, a monastery can be seen. Its temple stands in the middle, surrounded by monk dwellings. Down in the valley lies a nomadic campground, around which some yaks browse. Yaks are a type of Asian buffalo, typical of the Himalayan region. In the foreground, a village perches on a rocky cliff. It is dominated by the prince's palace at the top.

King Song-Tsan Gam-Po and his two wives are pictured.

King Thri-Song Deu-Tsen invited Padmasambhava and other Buddhist masters to teach their beliefs in Tibet.

During a period of persecution against Buddhism ordered by King Lang-Sarma, the Buddhist monk Vimalamitra entered the royal courtyard in disguise and began dancing. The king, curious to see what was happening, appeared at his window. Vimalamitra then killed him with a bow and arrow that he had hidden in the wide sleeves of his costume

existing religion of this nomadic and livestock-rearing society was called Bon. This was most likely a variation on the shamanism of Asia.

Under the guidance of Gar Tsan Dombu, a descendant of Song-Tsan Gam-Po, the Tibetan army defeated the Chinese army in battle in the seventh century A.D. For about a decade, Tibet surged to the role of a great Asian empire. But as early as the end of the seventh century A.D., Tibet's strength was decreasing. China then regained all of the territory it had lost. During the reign of Thri-Song Deu-Tsen (755-797) the country went through a new expansionist phase and annexed several territories to the east (all the way to today's Ladak) and others to the north, toward China.

The Arrival of Buddhism

At this time, Buddhism took a firm hold on Tibet. After reading some Buddhist texts, King Thri-Song Deu-Tsen asked several Buddhist masters from India to come to Tibet and teach their religion to the Tibetan people. Thus, some of the most renowned representatives of the Buddhist world of the eighth century came to Tibet Among them was Padmasambhava. He played an important role in spreading Buddhism in Tibet. Soon the doctrine of the Enlightened spread among the aristocracy and in the court.

However, the spread of the new religion also encountered strong resistance from the followers of the Bon cult. They tried in any way they could to restrain the spread of the Buddhist teachings. The tension this created would often burst into crowded public debates.

The most important event in the history of Buddhism's spread into Tibet is the foundation of the great Monastery of Samye. The monastery was built in the eighth century by Padmasambhava and other Buddhist masters from India. For the occasion, the first group of Tibetan Buddhist monks was ordained, and the most important texts of the religion were translated from the Indian Pali and Sanscrit languages. Within a few centuries, Buddhism was to become the true soul of Tibet and its people.

THE QIN AND HAN EMPIRES

The Qin Dynasty Unites All China

The first Chinese imperial dynasty was founded in 221 B.C. by Shi Huangdi (the "First Emperor"). He expanded his dominion from the state of Qin, northwest of the central plain, to all of China.

According to modern scholars of Chinese history, Shi Huangdi established China's first empire ruled by a central government. In doing this, he reorganized and used ideas taken from the ancient royal dynasties. He restored the unity of power and the religious authority of the monarch as it was during the Shang dynasty. He also proclaimed that isolation was necessary for a monarch. Through withdrawal, the emperor could be free of the distractions of minor daily events and the restlessness of the world. In this way, an emperor allowed for emptiness within himself, so that the forces of the universe could freely act through him.

The Legalist Doctrine

During the first empire, Legalism triumphed. As stated earlier, Legalism was a philosophy that emphasized authority and strict laws. These measures, which had been so effective in the Qin state, were applied throughout China. They included standardizing the writing system, currency, weights, measures, and the legal system. Moreover, a network of roads connecting the provinces with the capital Xianyang (near Xian, in the Shaanxi region) was created. All of the orders were sent off from Xianyang, and the emperor ordered that the palaces of the ancient princedoms, now subject to him, be rebuilt in the capital.

The structure of the government was based on a powerful army and an emphasis on development and commercial exchange. All attempts at opposition were harshly crushed. In 213 B.C., the first minister Li Si had all of the ancient texts burned (except for the martial-arts essays and technical books). He also ordered that all scholars who were using the knowledge of the past to resist the present system should be killed. This policy of control went hand in hand with the policy of conquest. The armies of Shi Huangdi pushed their way to the borders of today's Chinese territory.

Above: The Great Wall was built at the end of the third century B.C. Shi Huangdi joined together preexisting defensive walls, which had been built by the local lords at the time of the Warring States. This wall, built along China's northwestern border, formed an unbroken barrier against the invasions of the nomads. *Insert, middle:* This graffiti-fresco shows a clash between the Chinese and nomadic armies, and a hunting scene *(lower part)*. As seen in the artwork, horses were now being used. *Opposite page:* The main military strength of the empire was the infantry. This army of clay warriors was discovered in 1974 inside the burial tomb of Emperor Qin Shi Huangdi in Lintong, in the Shaanxi region.

The Han Dynasty

The Qin dynasty survived only a few years after Shi Huangdi's death. In 206 B.C., power passed into the hands of a new family, called Han. This family ruled over China until A.D. 220, but its reign was divided into two periods; that of the Former Han (206 B.C.-A.D. 8) and that of the Later Han (A.D. 25-220). During the middle period (A.D. 9-25), Wang Mang seized the throne and founded the Xin dynasty.

The development of the Han dynasty was somewhat similar to that of the Shang-Zhou dynasties. The emperors established their capital first in Changan to the west (in the Xian region), and then in Luoyang in the heart of the central plain (in the Henan region). The Han continued the politics of Shi Huangdi in its basic concepts, but they ruled with the scholars, and not against them. They also continued the expansionist policy. Kings or leaders who recognized the authority of the emperor were given a gold seal as a symbol of their local power.

Much more difficult were the relationships with the nomadic tribes of the Xiongnu. These tribes were constantly raiding the northwestern borders of China, which forced the empire to completely revise its defense system. The Great Wall had already been built by Shi Huangdi. His workers built the wall by joining fortresses built during the Zhou dynasty.

Inside the country, the Han dynasty alternately promoted the Legalist and Confucian ideas. These two schools of thought arose as a result of the chaos of the Warring States period, but they were often in conflict. For example, Legalists supported the state monopolies on staple items such as salt, iron, alcohol, and tea. The followers of Confucius preferred a more flexible system. The historical sources recorded all of these shifts. But they could not establish a direct relationship between the dominance of each doctrine and the corresponding economic situation (which was most often quite unstable).

In this period, a stable trading route connected the Mediterranean to China. It soon became a major channel of circulation for people, goods, and ideas. Later on, this route was to be called "the Silk Road."

This drum from the Han period was found in the southern regions which were becoming part of the Chinese Empire.

This clay boat model was found inside a tomb of the Later Han period, second century A.D.

The trading route, today called "the Silk Road," connected China with the Mediterranean, passing through central Asia, Persia, and Syria.

1) coins, 2) measure, 3) bronze weight. Shi Huangdi united the weight and measurement system throughout China.

Society in China During the Han Dynasty

The Dynastic Histories

During the Han period, scholars took an inventory of knowledge collected. Sima Qian (145-90 B.C.) gathered the first Dynastic History, and the structure he devised was to remain practically unchanged in all of the following twenty-one histories of China, from the beginning to the republic of this century.

The University: Cultural and Practical Education

The creation of the Imperial University in 124 B.C. was part of the line of thought of the time. The institution was meant to preserve the

This jade object comes from the Han period. It represents the bi disc, a symbol of the Sky.

intellectual history of the nation. But it was also meant to produce, after a period of studies, good servants for the state. The students, however, were chosen not only according to their intellectual skills, but also on the basis of some "new categories" of qualities or faults which were credited to them by a jury of wise men.

The Way of Life Must Reflect the Social Conditions

During the Han dynasty, rules concerning the proper use of luxury items were set. Material possessions were the means through which each individual was given a rightful place in the society. This rule applied to everyone, from the imperial princes (who had survived the advent of the Han dynasty and lost all powers on their lands in the first century B.C.) down to the members of the government, including the state ministers and the "kings" (rulers of the great central plain, whose authority was confirmed by the emperor but subject to his confirmation). The administrators of the provinces, prefects, and sub-prefects had to live according to their degree of rank. The *History of the Later Han* (Hou Hansu) gives a firsthand account on the proper use of clothes and vehicles in imperial China. Vehicles, in particular, were an important symbol of a person's prestige.

Jade Shrouds and Burials

Another area where ritual was applied with extreme strictness was that of funerals. Burials were often organized by the person in his or her lifetime. They also exactly reflected one's social

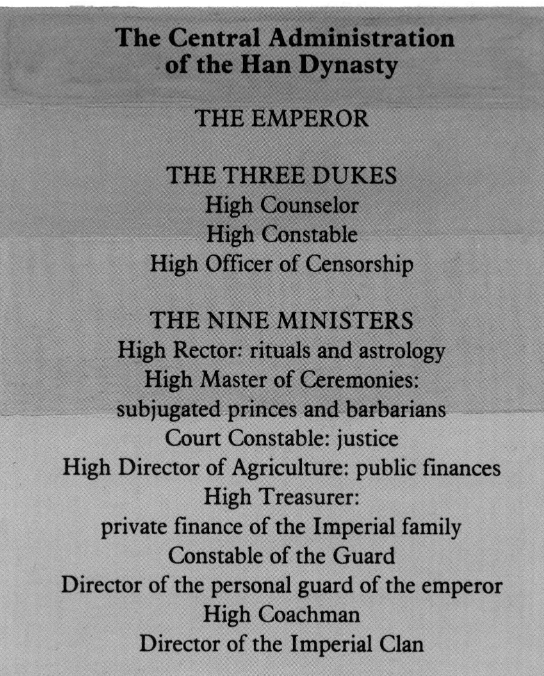

The Central Administration of the Han Dynasty

THE EMPEROR

THE THREE DUKES
High Counselor
High Constable
High Officer of Censorship

THE NINE MINISTERS
High Rector: rituals and astrology
High Master of Ceremonies: subjugated princes and barbarians
Court Constable: justice
High Director of Agriculture: public finances
High Treasurer: private finance of the Imperial family
Constable of the Guard
Director of the personal guard of the emperor
High Coachman
Director of the Imperial Clan

condition. The tombs of the Han nobles, of which several well-preserved examples exist, reached heights of splendor. The most beautiful are those of the Imperial Prince Liu Sheng and his wife Touwan in Mancheng (in the Hebei region).

Each corpse was actually enclosed in armor made of over two thousand jade tiles tied together with gold thread. This kind of shroud was used only during the Former Han period (206 B.C.-A.D. 8). It was supposed to prevent the decomposition of the body according to a belief going back to the Neolithic age. The *Dynastic Histories* mention these shrouds more than once, and archaeologists have discovered more than twenty of them. They were always used to cover the bodies of people related to the imperial family. But even in this, a hierarchy was clearly defined. The threads holding the jade tiles together could be made of bronze, silver, or gold, thus revealing the social status of the dead.

This drawing recreates the pavilion of an aristocratic residence of the Han period. Inside can be seen, from bottom to top: the servants at work; men at a meeting; women in conversation.

Below: During the Han period, lacquered wood came to be used even for tableware. This very elegant set was found in a tomb at Mawangdui which dates from 160 B.C.

This scene captures life in a village. In the foreground, a weaver works a pedal-driven loom, such as those constructed in the epoch.

Below: A plan for the tomb of Prince Liu Sheng (154-113 B.C.) was discovered at Mancheng in 1968. The main areas are: **1)** access corridor, **2)** antechamber, **3)** carriage house and stable, **4)** central chamber, **5)** mortuary chamber, and **6)** bathhouse.

The funeral vestments of the Princess Touwan, wife of Liu Sheng, were made of jade tiles held together with a network of gold thread.

Nomads invade a Chinese town. Such events were frequent in the northern territories, which were threatened by steppe populations moving toward the plains of the Huang He.

The Yangtze River flows through a southern landscape. In this period, the southern territories gave shelter to refugees from the north and regained the importance which they had lost at the time of the Han Empire. ODO

THE THREE KINGDOMS AND THE SIX DYNASTIES

The Fall of the Han Empire

After its brilliant beginning as the glory of the ancient world, the Han Empire fell into chaos in the third century A.D. It was a society on the verge of collapse. In particular, the society suffered from economic chaos. Neither Confucians nor Legalists knew how to handle the economy which wavered between liberalism and government control. The economy was further weakened by long cycles of severe weather.

There was also military chaos, and invading nomads pressed upon the frontiers. For nearly half a century (from A.D. 220-265), the Chinese territory was partitioned among the "Three Kingdoms" (Wei, Shu, and Wu). During this time, the rule of the "Six Dynasties" (A.D. 222-589) began in the south. For a short time, China's unity was restored under the rule of the Western Jin dynasty (A.D. 265-316), but the country had been devastated. It wasn't long before nomad invaders conquered northern China. In the period that followed, the northern territory was divided into many smaller states ruled by an ever-changing succession of rulers. Meanwhile, in southern China, the Jin dynasty remained in power. Gradually the situation stabilized; four dynasties succeeded each other in the southern territories, while the north was first ruled by the Northern Wei (A.D. 386-534), then by the Western Wei (A.D. 534-550).

Intellectual Crisis and the Spread of Modern Buddhism

On top of the division of the country came a deep intellectual crisis. Traditional Chinese thought no longer seemed capable of explaining life so threatened in those dark times. What solution was offered to the dreaded problem of death? Chinese thinkers, the Daoists in particular, had devised complicated theories, invented methods for the survival of the spirit, and imagined lands of delight—true paradises only

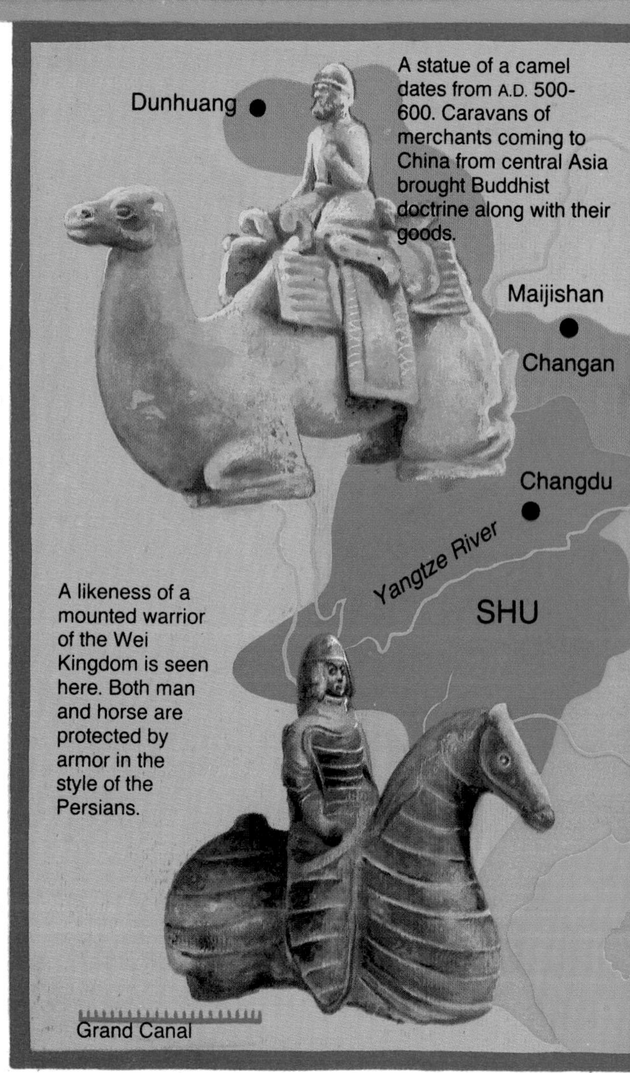

A statue of a camel dates from A.D. 500-600. Caravans of merchants coming to China from central Asia brought Buddhist doctrine along with their goods.

A likeness of a mounted warrior of the Wei Kingdom is seen here. Both man and horse are protected by armor in the style of the Persians.

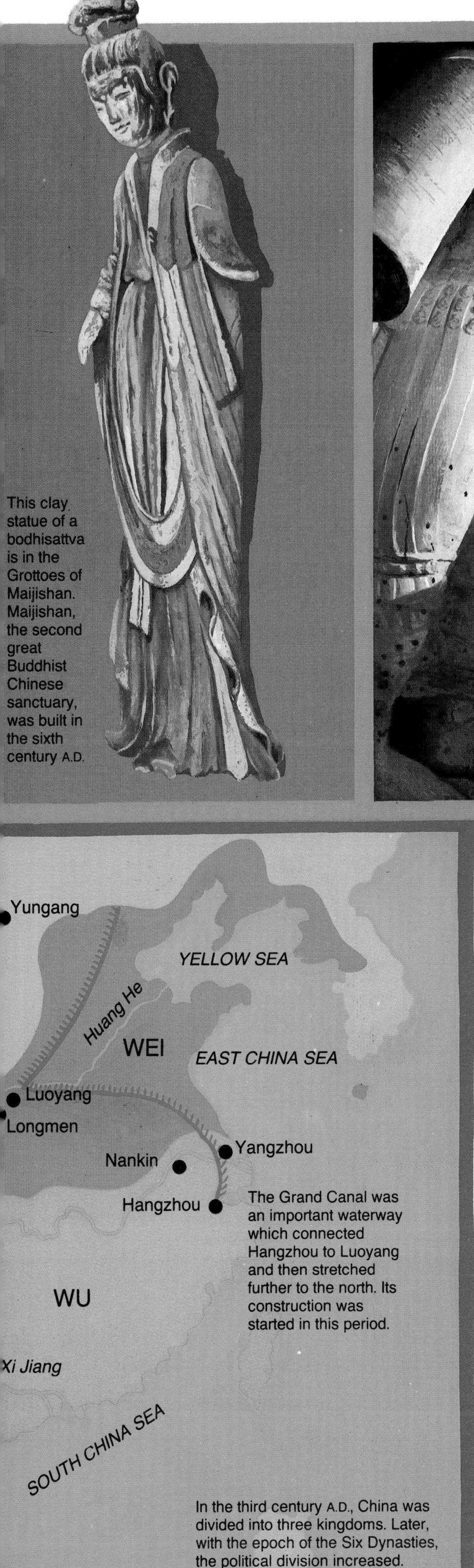

This clay statue of a bodhisattva is in the Grottoes of Maijishan. Maijishan, the second great Buddhist Chinese sanctuary, was built in the sixth century A.D.

The Grand Canal was an important waterway which connected Hangzhou to Luoyang and then stretched further to the north. Its construction was started in this period.

In the third century A.D., China was divided into three kingdoms. Later, with the epoch of the Six Dynasties, the political division increased.

The rock-sanctuary of Yungang, with its giant Buddha, was built by the monks between A.D. 460 and 495.

In China, the building which contains relics of the Buddha is called a pagoda. The pagoda of the Temple of the White Horse in Luoyang is seen here. This was the first Buddhist temple to be built in China.

available to those who had saved themselves. But what about the common people? At this point, a new teaching brought by travelers and foreign merchants spread into China. It was Buddhism that taught the highest control of passions.

Before true Chinese Buddhism could develop, however, it was necessary to translate the basic texts of this doctrine. When this was done, the Chinese thinkers started to get acquainted with completely new concepts, such as that of nothingness. The adaptation to this different way of thinking took place within small intellectual circles. In southern China, the intellectual circles were especially active, and a spiritual way of life of pure Chinese tradition was flourishing.

At this point, China was divided into two spiritual zones with differences that were stressed by the traditional Chinese scholars. Northern China was more rational, believing in the Confucian virtues of teaching and in the efforts necessary for gradual "discovery" of truth. Southern China was more mystical and Daoist oriented and believed that enlightenment could be attained only in an instantaneous and global way. This geographical and philosophical split was triggered by the arrival of Buddhism. It was soon felt as a fact of life throughout the nation and was applied to all fields of knowledge.

The Buddhist Rock-Sanctuaries

During this period, sanctuaries rose all over the country. The most extraordinary among them were the rock-sanctuaries. These small sanctuaries or cells were dug in cliffs gathered around a huge image of the Buddha. These sanctuaries rose along all of the trading routes which connected the Far East with the Mediterranean, on both sides of Pamir.

The most ancient rock-sanctuaries in China are the Sanctuary of Dunhuan dating back to the end of the fourth century, Maijishan, Yungang, and Longmen. The last two contain the best examples of religious Chinese sculpture. The style of Chinese sculpture was at first influenced by Indian standards, then tended to become more graphical and stylized.

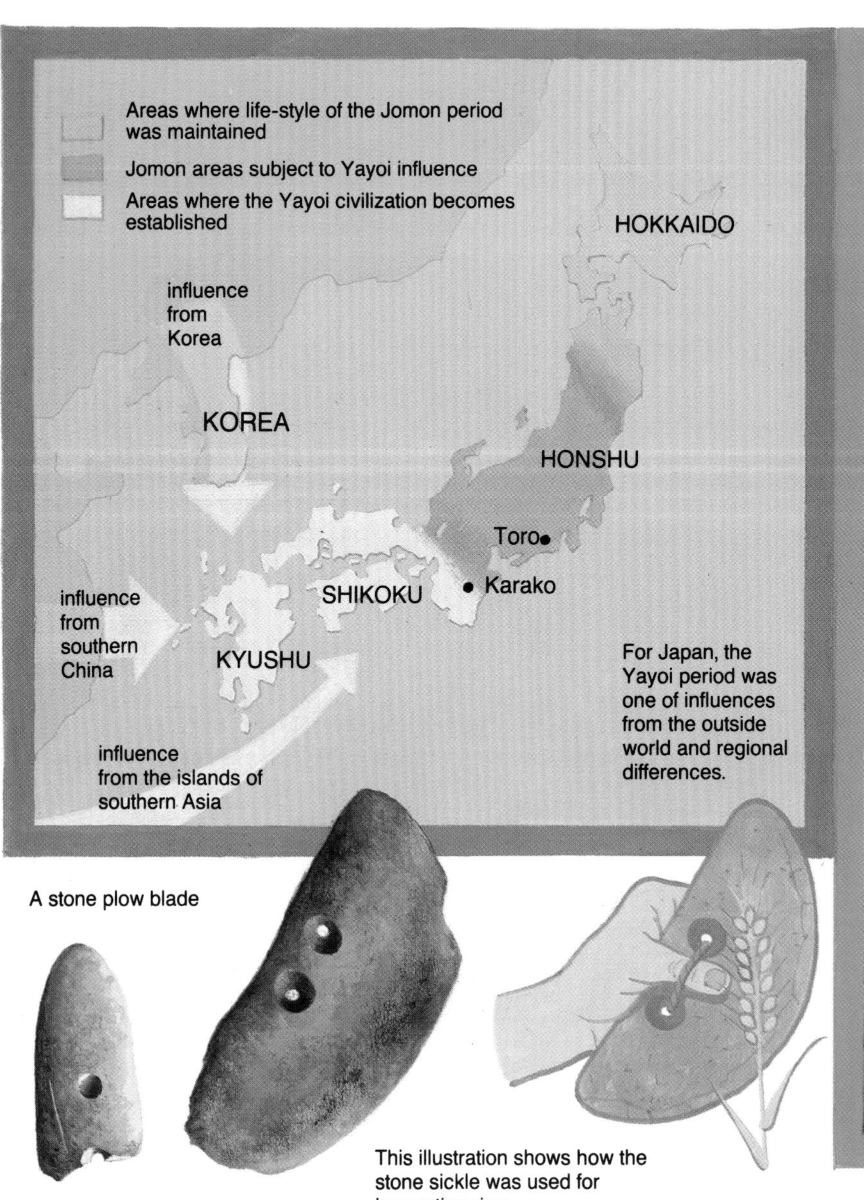

For Japan, the Yayoi period was one of influences from the outside world and regional differences.

A stone plow blade

This illustration shows how the stone sickle was used for harvesting rice.

A typical village of the Yayoi epoch

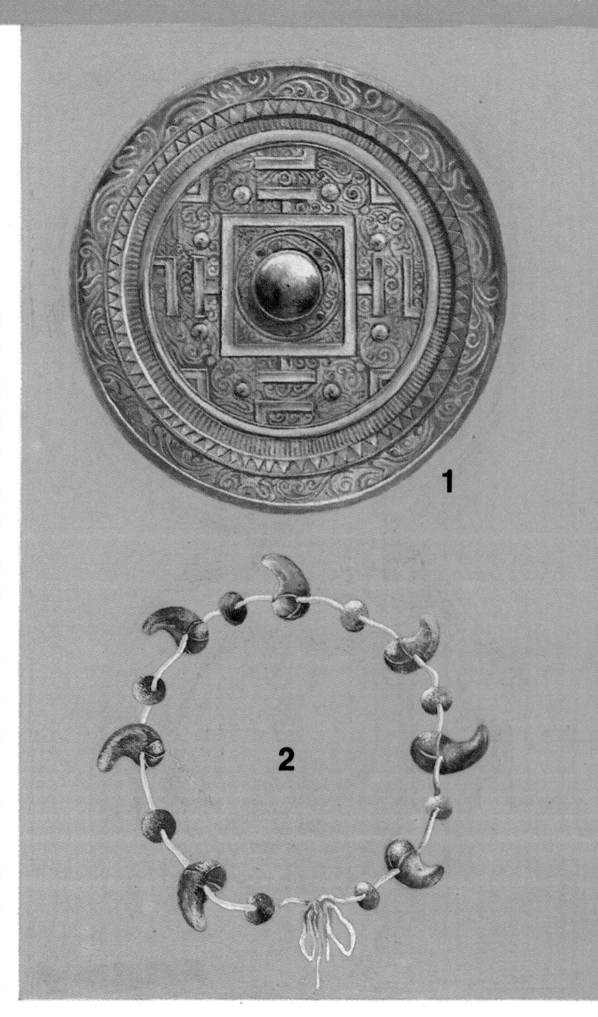

Agriculture and Bronze in Japan: The Yayoi Epoch

The Late Jomon Period and the First Hints of Agriculture

During the middle Jomon period (roughly 1500-1000 B.C.) many technological changes occurred in Japan. The people who cut stone, bone, and wood skillfully perfected their hunting and fishing tools. They invented the harpoon with a mobile point and started catching large fish. They also improved the system of weights and buoys that had been used on nets for five hundred years. The potters also showed great creativity. They created ceramics which had new shapes and patterns. Their work was an imitation, or a distant echo, of the complex metal vases being created by the Chinese workers in bronze during the same period.

In the middle Jomon period, a primitive form of agriculture developed on land freed of forest by fire. Only in the late Jomon period (around 1000-500 B.C.) did rice cultivation begin. Many ceramic remains of the late Jomon period have rice impressions on their bottoms, particularly the ones from the northern region of the island of Kyushu. Rice cultivation on flooded fields had been introduced from the middle and lower reaches of the Yangtze River (China), where rice fields had existed since 5000 B.C. Only around 300 B.C. did rice cultivation begin on a large scale in Japan, corresponding with the spread of the metal civilization.

Within a few years, agriculture fully developed in Japan. At the same time, the potter's wheel had come into use, and metal-bearing minerals were being collected and processed. Together, these improvements marked the beginning of a new culture in Japan. This culture, called Yayoi, started in Kyushu. The name *Yayoi* refers to the part of Tokyo in which pottery from this time was first discovered.

The new culture eventually spread east until

A corpse inside a jar was buried beneath a dolmen according to the custom of the Yayoi epoch.

To the left: These ritual bronze objects were owned by the chief: **1)** mirror **2)** necklace with magatama, stones in the shape of a tiger's claws **3)** two large-bladed halberds **4)** clapperless bell.

Above, to the left: Use of the potter's wheel, which created vases such as this one, changed the appearance of Japanese ceramics.

Above: This vase, decorated with human features, is rather unusual for its time.

it reached Honshu, the largest of the Japanese islands. But the movement was very slow and left whole areas untouched. In the regions of the northeast, the people continued a Jomon life-style for many more centuries. These people only began to conform to the life-style of central Japan in the ninth century A.D.

The Rice Economy

Rice-growing was one of the most important advances gained from the Yayoi epoch. Rice-growing led to a stable life-style and required a stronger sense of community than did other cultures. For this reason, it seems that each village was ruled by a chief, very often a shaman woman. In the villages of Karako (in the Nara Prefecture) and Toro (in the Shizuoka Prefecture), rice is still grown today very much like it was grown in the past.

At this time, religion and cult were probably more important than war. Weapons were made, but a large quantity of the bronze artifacts from this period are not very practical. Items such as mirrors, halberds, spatula-shaped spears, and clapperless bells were probably used for rituals.

The variety of religious beliefs is evident in the many types of burials. Some people were buried inside large ceramic jars, with single or double walls, while others were buried in stone coffins. By the end of the period, the burial sites were marked by dolmens. A dolmen is a large, flat stone, placed on a few vertical stones which were similar to those used in Korea during the same period. At the end of the Bronze Age, the Korean culture was a definite influence in Japan. This occurred because the two countries lie close together, and the various connecting islands made exchanges possible in spite of a dangerous sea.

The Epoch of the Ancient Tombs

The First Written Information on Japan

Japan appeared for the first time in the *Dynastic Histories of China* in the third century A.D. It was spoken of in the report of a journey undertaken around A.D. 240 by the ambassadors of the Chinese court of Wei, the dynasty which reigned over northern China (during the epoch of the Three Kingdoms). The travelers had explored the seas east of China and reported on the lands and the peoples they had met. They called the Japanese by the name of *woren*, meaning "dwarfs." On the other hand, they described in great detail the country's natural wealth and the civilization which flourished around the end of the Bronze Age. From this report, scholars have an account of the great Japanese towns and cemeteries, and of the village leaders, who were often women.

The Introduction of Iron and the Tombs

Between the third and fourth centuries, Japan began to work iron, making its own tools and weapons. The changes caused by this development were profound. With it came a new concept of power. The great burial mounds of the emperors Ijin and Nintoku (fifth century) and the impressive remains of ancient Japan found in today's Osaka are evidence of this. Many of these tombs are still part of the Japanese landscape today. Covered with round, square, or "lock-shaped" mounds, they protected the bodies of the military leaders.

Each body was placed in a sarcophagus (stone coffin), dressed in full armor. Full armor included an iron and leather cuirass (a piece of armor that covered the body from neck to waist), a helmet, gold and jade jewels, a quiver, arrows, and swords. Sometimes the swords had inscriptions on them. These inscriptions are Japan's most ancient examples of writing. Besides iron weapons, though, these warriors owned another extraordinary thing: horses. The warrior's horses were as richly adorned as the warrior was.

Gold earrings and the gold-plated bronze headgear and footwear of a prince were found in Funeyama (Kumamoto Prefecture).

The map shows where the objects discussed on these two pages were found.

A mural from the tomb of Takehara (prefecture of Fukuoka) depicts a man, two horses, and palms. *Opposite page:* The great royal tombs, shaped like door locks, are found in the region of Osaka.

These tombs, like the great Chinese tombs, were guarded by replicas of servants, animals, and various miniature objects. These clay models accompanied the dead and also had a practical purpose. They helped to stabilize the mound of dirt raised above the tomb. The walls inside the tombs, especially in the northern Kyushu region, were also richly decorated. Some had paintings of geometrical patterns, while others had scenes whose meanings are obscure.

The discovery of iron greatly changed the Japanese life-style. The new feeling of power it inspired also gave rise to a new ruling class. According to the Japanese histories compiled from the eighth century on, this class was very enterprising. In A.D. 369, these knights were attracted to Korea, from which many artisans and wise men had come into Japan. The warriors sailed to the Korean peninsula and founded a small Japanese colony, the Mimana state, which lasted for about two centuries. Today, the Korean scholars dispute the existence of this ancient Japanese colony.

The Emperor and the Court of Yamato

The new authority of the war commander eclipsed that of the shaman. From these innovations, the concept of the emperor was born in Japan. The emperor was the symbol of the country and was above all earthly matters. He survived all changes and revolutions.

The historical creation of the Japanese nation has been placed in the fourth century. It is symbolized by the existence of the "Court of Yamato." This was formed in today's prefecture of Nara, on the Yamato plateau. In the beginning, it was only a small clan, but it was more powerful than the neighboring clans and perhaps more receptive to the new forms of thought and technology that were coming from the continent. From this clan, came the ancestors of the imperial family.

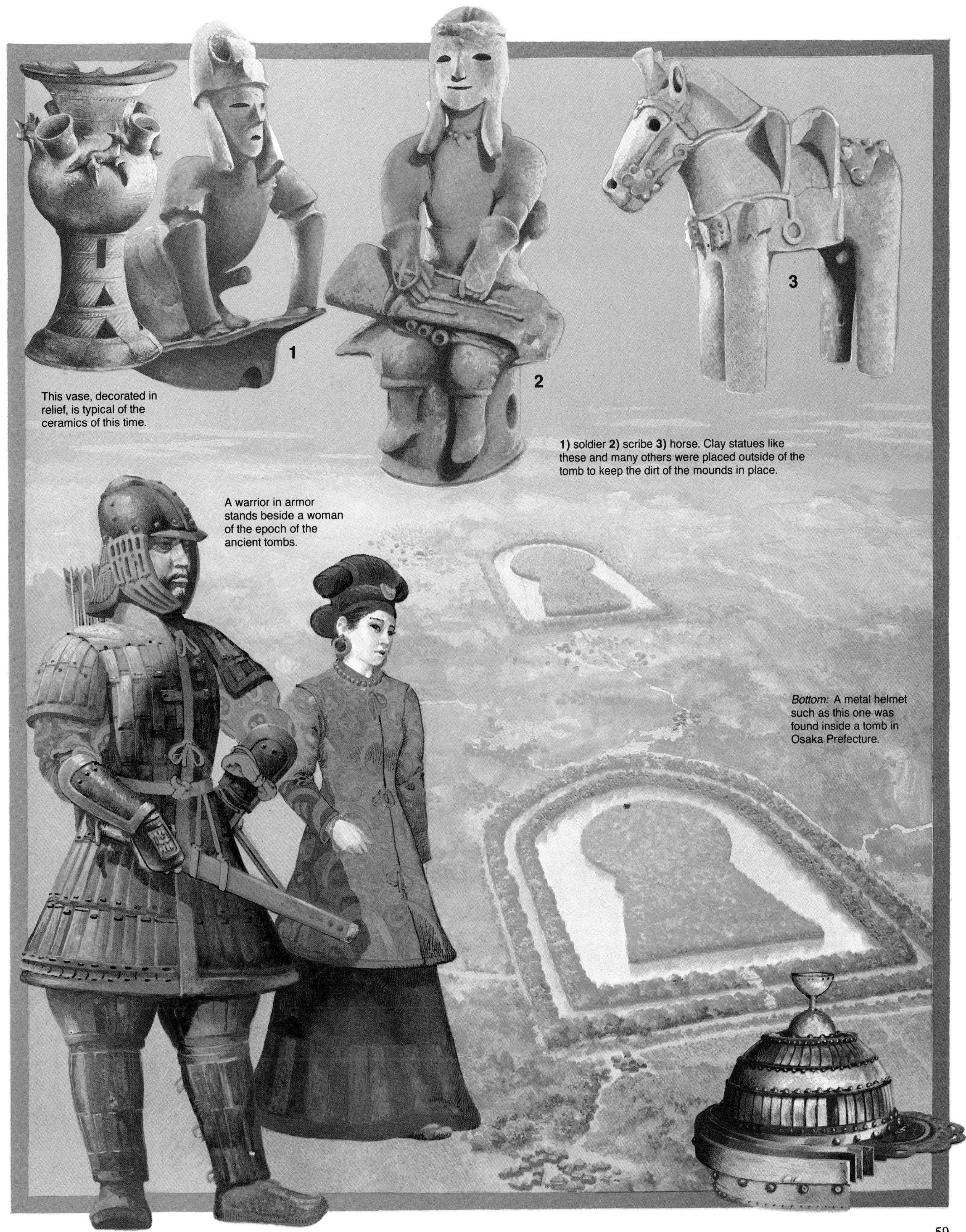

This vase, decorated in relief, is typical of the ceramics of this time.

1) soldier **2)** scribe **3)** horse. Clay statues like these and many others were placed outside of the tomb to keep the dirt of the mounds in place.

A warrior in armor stands beside a woman of the epoch of the ancient tombs.

Bottom: A metal helmet such as this one was found inside a tomb in Osaka Prefecture.

JAPAN MODERNIZES

More Monumental Tombs

The Yamato plateau is considered the historical heart of ancient Japan. In the fifth century A.D., the plateau was dotted by hundreds of burial mounds. Some of these artificial mountains were up to 984 feet (300 m) long and were surrounded by one or two moats. The custom of building these mounds became an important tradition in the prominent families. It lasted for at least two more centuries. Finally, Emperor Kotoku (who reigned from A.D. 645 to 654) issued a decree limiting such expensive burials. In spite of it, the mounds were built until the eighth century, as the tombs of Takamatsuzuka attest. The paintings on their walls were reproductions of other paintings in Chinese tombs of the same time. The fact that burial rituals continued throughout many centuries leads scholars to think that, in spite of political and technological changes, power did not change hands. Instead, the ancient clans grew increasingly stronger from their ability to endure.

The Introduction of Buddhism

In this period, Japan was by no means isolated. It was open to all foreign influences, including those of Korea and its artisans who fled the disruption caused by nomadic tribes in northern China. It also absorbed the elements of Chinese civilization at a time when that civilization was flourishing. Around the middle of the sixth century (traditionally in A.D. 538 or 552), the Buddhist religion reached Japan. With it came the Sutra, which contained Buddhists teachings, and the Chinese writing which the Japanese strove to adapt to their language.

The introduction of Buddhist religion was not readily accepted by all of the Japanese people. In fact, not all of the clans were converted to the new religion. Some, such as the Mononobe and the Nakatomi, resisted actively. They called Buddhism ill-fated, foreign thought and believed it to be unsuitable for Japan. Meanwhile, other clans, under the banner of the Soga, declared it necessary to adapt to the Chinese thinking. Chinese technology was already practiced by Korean artisans, and their skills were well known. To the Soga clans, these skills were proof of the value of the doctrine which inspired them. This resulted in a war between the supporters of the country's tradition and the supporters of openness to foreign ideas. The emperor's role was vital at this point. He favored the Soga's views and did not hesitate to turn down

Regent Shotoku is responsible for modernizing Japan between the sixth and seventh centuries A.D. He is seen here in a famous representation with two of his ministers. The different heights correspond to the differing importance of the figures.

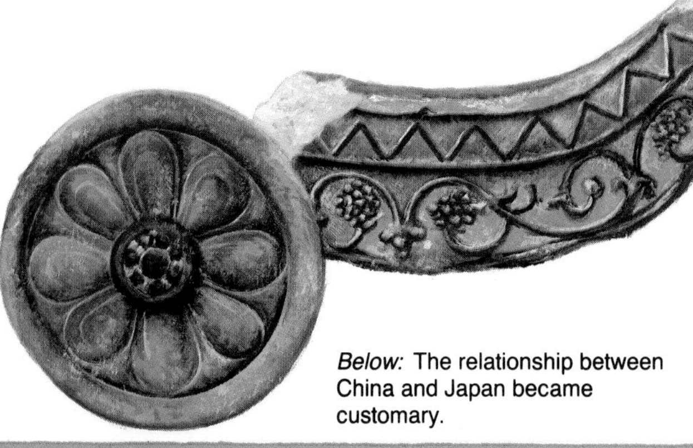

To the left: These ornamental clay pieces are part of a tile roof. Tile roofing was introduced into Japan at this time. *To the right:* The stone foundations are all that remain of many of the early Japanese buildings. Here, the remains of columns stand in the location of the Dazaifu palace. This southern city served the administration as an important seat for dealing with China and the continent.

Below: The relationship between China and Japan became customary.

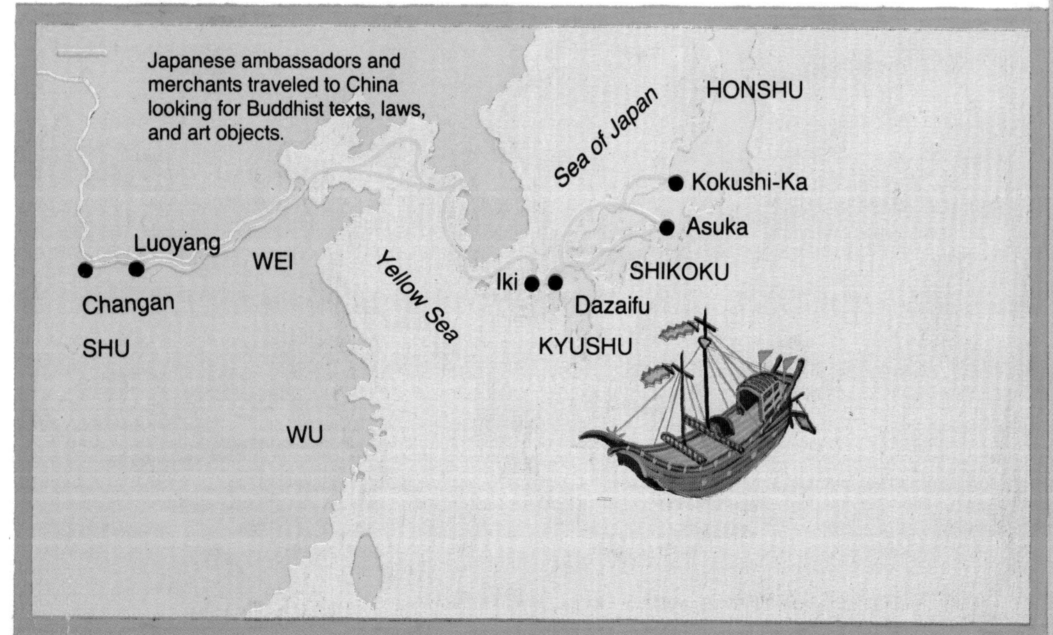

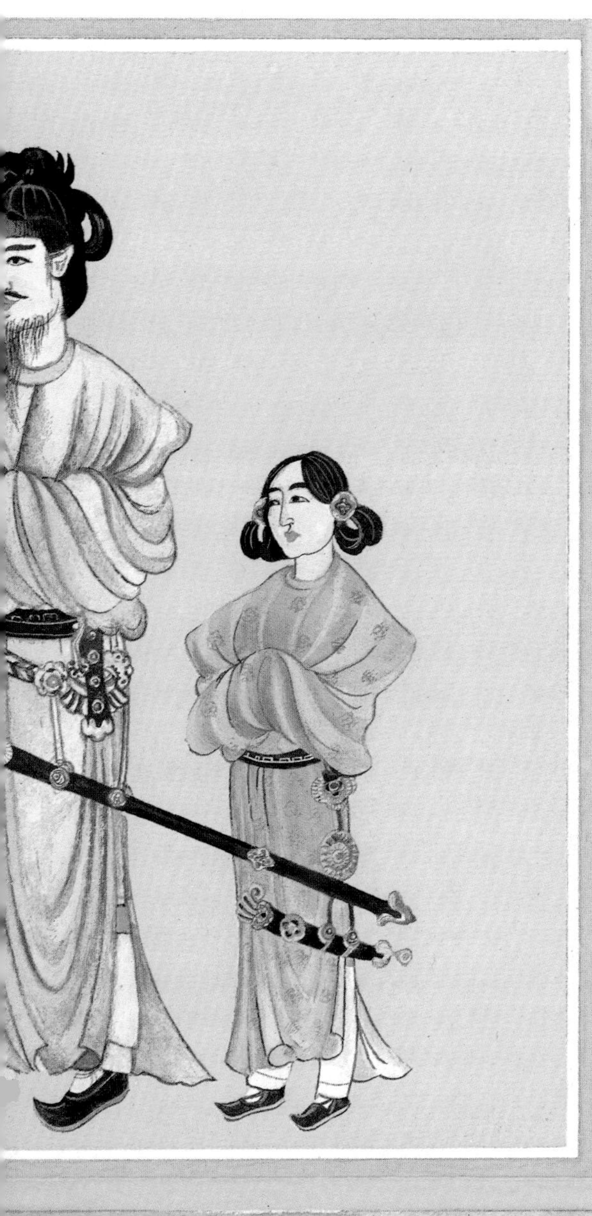

advice from the most important religious and military people in his court. It was a difficult struggle. Finally, after violent clashes and failures, the Soga clan and other supporters of Buddhism were victorious in A.D. 587.

The Regent Shotoku

A few years later, in 592, Empress Suiko ascended the throne and reigned until 628. A tireless woman, Suiko worked toward the modernization of Japan and brilliantly initiated a series of female rulers. Suiko gave herself the Chinese title of "Celestial Sovereign." She granted all powers to her nephew, Prince Shotoku (574-622), appointing him regent.

As regent, Shotoku reorganized the government. In 603, he established twelve court ranks. The ranks, separated by different colored hats, made the different functions of each clear. A year later, in 604, he gave Japan the Seventeen Article Constitution. In it, Shotoku organized ideals for government and for individual conduct. The constitution, like the twelve rank court system, clearly defined the duties and rights of the ruler, the ministers, and the people.

In addition, Regent Shotoku also tried to devise a regular measure of time, the only way history could be recorded. In the same year in which the constitution was written, the ages began to be computed according to Chinese custom, starting from a fixed point which the emperor would redefine from time to time. To complete his work, Regent Shotoku opened relations with China.

The Taika Reform

Regent Shotoku's ideas encouraged Japan's modernization. These ideas were met with much resistance from people who feared the power of a centralized government. It was not until the Taika epoch (645-649) that many of these ideas became a reality. During this epoch, the new emperor and his suporters perfected modernication program called the Taika Reform. This program ended private land ownership. All land was turned over to the state, redivided, and parceled out again. The new landowners were allowed to farm the land, for which they paid a set tax.

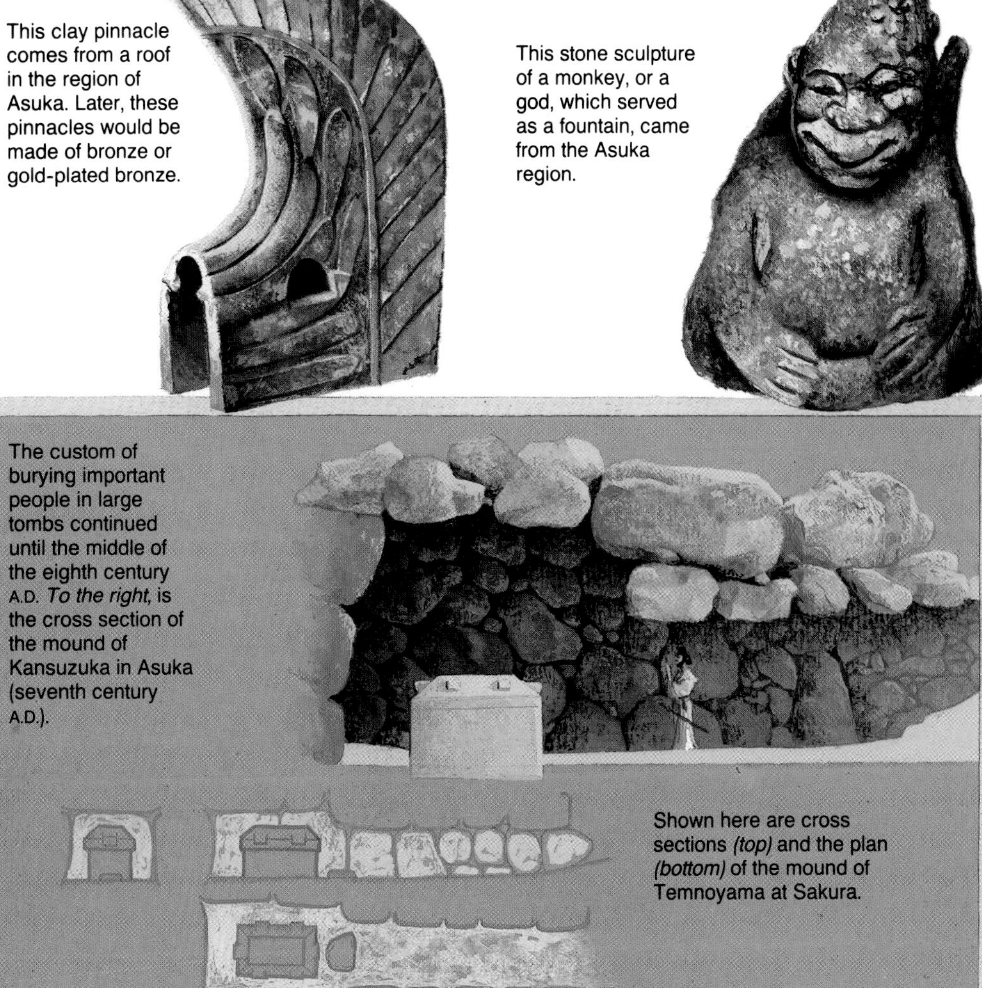

This clay pinnacle comes from a roof in the region of Asuka. Later, these pinnacles would be made of bronze or gold-plated bronze.

This stone sculpture of a monkey, or a god, which served as a fountain, came from the Asuka region.

The custom of burying important people in large tombs continued until the middle of the eighth century A.D. *To the right,* is the cross section of the mound of Kansuzuka in Asuka (seventh century A.D.).

Shown here are cross sections *(top)* and the plan *(bottom)* of the mound of Temnoyama at Sakura.

Top: Izumo is one of the two oldest Shintoist sanctuaries in Japan. It is located on the coast of the Japan Sea, at a site where ships from Korea and China were sure to seek harbor. The square plan of the sanctuary, with the entrance off-center and to the right, is seen at the top right.

THE RELIGIONS OF JAPAN

The Tradition of Animism

The ancient religion of Japan was a natural cult called animism. The term *animism* was first used by British anthropologist Edward B. Tylor in his theory on the origin of religion. Animism refers to any religion in which spirits are of central importance. These spirits are often the souls of dead people. Other spirits are found in the natural world. Animism's followers often worship natural forces such as the sun, thunder, the wind, and life in all its forms, both animal and vegetable.

Shinto

The roots of Shinto, which is the oldest religion still practiced in Japan, go back to the Bronze and Iron ages. The word *Shinto* literally means "the way of the kami." *Kami* means "gods," but it historically refers to beings who are superior to humans. Shinto followers worship many kami, who are found in natural forces. Eventually, this reverence extended to the dead, who are also considered higher beings than humans.

The Japanese gave great importance to the concept of purity, both physical and moral. Little by little, great purification rituals were developed, with the objective of putting society back in order. The highest priest of this religion was the acknowledged leader of the clans, the emperor.

The shinto ritual was brought to the peak of its sacredness with the construction of two sanctuaries, the oldest in Japan. Ise, east of the Yamato region, faced the sun and was the most properly imperial sanctuary since it housed the "Three Jewels"—the mirror, the sword, and

A large stone statue of two gods, a male and a female, was used to cover a fountain in the Asuka region.

Above: The legend and reality of the foundation of a temple is depicted in this drawing. Following the directions given to the emperor in a dream, the imperial messengers go to the location chosen. There, laborers and carpenters start construction with spirit. The drawing was inspired by various paintings from the fourteenth and sixteenth centuries A.D.

Far above: The Buddhist sanctuary of Horyuji is located in Nara. To the left is the pagoda, containing the relics of the Buddha. To the right is the kondo, which is the main body of the temple, where the sacred image is preserved. At the top left corner is the plan for the sanctuary, which includes the cloister and other secondary buildings where the monks lived.

To the left: The famous iron sword of the seven points is considered the most ancient imperial symbol known in Japan. The length of the sword is decorated with gold inscriptions in Chinese.

the pearl. These were the symbols of the mystical and political power of the emperor. Izumo, which faced north toward Korea, was built on the shore of the Sea of Japan. Together the two temples reflect the oriental concept of a dual world, male versus female, light versus darkness, as was similarly explained in China by the image of the alternating Yin and Yang.

In Japan, the union of the Shinto with the concept of the emperor began an important mythological cycle. This cycle centered around two characters: Amaterasu-o mikami, the Sun Goddess, source of all forms of life and founder of the imperial family; and Susanoo, her brother, the Lord of Darkness, the muddler and destroyer. An entire series of tales sprung up around this brother and sister, telling the story of the world's creation.

Buddhism and Its Temples

As seen in the previous chapter, Buddhism's influence became very strong in Japan between A.D. 500 and 700. This growth was due in part to the approval granted to this religion by the emperors. In his reform plan, Regent Shotoku attached great importance to religion as an element of unity and modernization of the country. In 594, he chose Buddhism as the national religion, following the spiritual guidance of the empress.

Shinto and Buddhism

Throughout the centuries, Shinto and Buddhism existed side by side, each one following its own path. Shinto, hostile to ideas coming from the continent, opposed the culture of the powerful Chinese neighbors. Because of this, the existence of Shinto guaranteed that the identity of the Japanese people would live on.

To unify the people's strength, Buddhism had to accept the spiritual value of the Shinto religion. Despite the acceptance of Shinto, Buddhism remained of great importance in Japanese life and is so even today. The coexistence of these two religions is evidence of Japan's ability to create harmony from conflicting elements, one of its main characteristics.

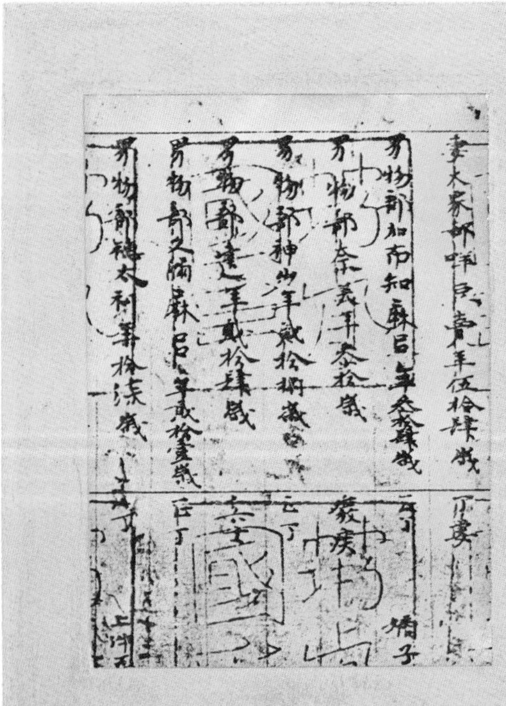

Pictured here is a codex dating from the Taiho epoch in A.D. 701. A codex is an ancient manuscript of historical importance. This is the oldest Japanese codex known today. This document was important in helping scholars understand early Japanese writing.

A detail of elaborate decoration was preserved in the temple of Horyuji in the town of Nara. The painting shows three moments of an event in the Buddha's life. The Enlightened takes off his clothes and throws himself off a cliff. At the bottom, he offers his body to a tiger and its offspring out of compassion for the starving creatures and any other living being.

THE BIRTH OF JAPANESE ART

The Main Innovations

Changes occurred in the social and religious structure of Japan between the sixth and seventh centuries. Signs of these changes were especially apparent in the arts and architecture. All over the country, Chinese culture affected local tradition. Chinese-style houses with lacquered columns and tiled roofs replaced buildings of the ancient Yayoi society. In the new religions, bronze statues replaced traditional stone statues. Even the costumes worn during official ceremonies were adapted from Chinese ceremonial clothes.

Painting

Only a few traces of the ancient paintings remain today. They are mainly decorations in old tombs, especially in the northern Kyushu region, consisting of simple shapes and symbols. But a major change occurred in 603. At that time, Regent Shotoku granted an official status to the Korean and Chinese artists. He entrusted them with the task of decorating the newly built temples. Thus the famous paintings of Horyuji came to be. After some decades, the Japanese artists were able to equal or out perform their masters.

Sculpture

Buddhist sculpture, a new art, was also favored by the government's policy of protection and patronage. The empress Suiko, or the regent Shotoku, commissioned the first works. The statues were mainly made of bronze. Some were then gold-plated; others were left plain, under the direction of a family of artisans of Chinese-Korean origin, the Tori family.

Among the more famous works is "Triad of Sakyamuni," which was preserved in Nara. The figures in this work are frontally positioned and elongated, a typical feature of the artwork of the Northern Wei in China. From the Korean artists, the Japanese artists also learned a different way of depicting their subjects, with more attention to smooth, rounded forms. To this, they added a rare grace, which can be perceived in the wooden statues—where the subjects are sculpted from a single piece of wood. Examples of this include the Buddha of the future, preserved in the Chuguji temple of the Horyuji sanctuary, or the statues of the Koryuji temple in Kyoto.

Literature

The first existing written works in Japanese date from the early 700s. Prior to the arrival of the Chinese in Japan, there was no written form of Japanese. The Japanese adapted Chinese writing to create their own written language. Basically, a character in Chinese represents a whole word. The Japanese used Chinese characters to represent sounds in Japanese. Thus, a Japanese word of four syllables was written with four Chinese characters—even though those characters might have represented four separate words in Chinese. This system made Japanese writing very cumbersome, and it was difficult to learn. For a long time, only educated Japanese could read their language. As time passed, changes made to Japanese writing made it more appropriate to the spoken language.

The oldest written works in Japanese are two historical works written in 712 and 720. The first work of literature was the *Man'yoshu.* That was a collection of over 4,000 poems. The first fiction was written in the tenth century. Japan's greatest novel, written by a woman, dates from the early eleventh century.

The Triad of Sakyamuni is a bronze sculpture depicting the Buddha between two lesser figures. Created in A.D. 823, this sculpture is the most important image of the temple of Horyuji. It is the work of the sculptor Tori.

These three bronze, gold-plated statuettes are part of a group of forty-eight, called "The Birth of Buddha." These sculptures, created in the eighth century A.D., are also from the temple of Horyuji.

This wooden statue shows a Buddha of the future, benevolent and invincible, in the meditation position. It is believed to have been commissioned by the Regent Shotoku. It is preserved in the temple of Koryuji in Kyoto and dates back to the seventh century A.D.

The wooden head of a Buddha of the future was found in the temple of Horyuji in Nara.

A close-up captures the head of the Buddha statue in Kyoto. Notice that the hairstyle is in the flattened, tricorn Korean style.

The main sites of the Bronze Age are shown on the map.

In villages on the coast of southeast Asia, farming activities were complemented with fishing and trade. These activities were made possible by the construction of better boats, hollowed with the help of bronze tools.

THE LONG BRONZE AGE IN SOUTHEAST ASIA

Bronze and the Dong Civilization

At the beginning of the first millennium B.C., bronze appeared rather suddenly in the Neolithic societies of Indochina. Knowledge of the new metal came from China. People in Burma and Malaya, however, may have learned of it from India. Compared to the use of stone, the use of bronze was limited at first. But it rapidly spread and became predominant.

The regions under China's influence were the starting point for the spread of bronze throughout southeast Asia. Many bronze objects were found near the village of Dong Son, and the name of the site is used to identify the populations which best absorbed the new technique. These populations lived along the coasts of the Indochinese peninsula. The use of bronze tools improved the quality of the boats that these people used for fishing and trade. Taking advantage of the shallow waters of the internal seas and of the closeness of various islands, these peoples sailed all over the South China Sea and even reached part of the more southern seas.

Among the artifacts of this culture, bronze objects were predominant: lance heads, daggers, situlas, beautifully shaped vases. Ceramic and bone objects were also used. The detailed decorations were often of geometric patterns, but sometimes human figures were used. The most typical objects of the Dong Son civilization were large bronze drums, which were used in rituals and religious ceremonies. They are exceptional works of art for their size, sense of balance, and for the beauty of their decorations.

The Spread of the Dong Son Populations

Very little is known about the political life of this Bronze Age civilization. Only the archaeological finds indicate the extent of its spread. Certainly, the Dong Son people reached the south. They settled in Samrong Sen, Cambodia, along the Tembeling River, and reached Sumatra.

The Dong Son populations are responsible for the spread of bronze in Indonesia. At first, bronze was spread only in the form of traded items. Later, the actual techniques were taught to the people, inspiring the development of local production.

Above is a bronze drum of the Dong Son culture.

In the northern area of the Dong Son civilization, the ever-growing influence from China gave rise to the Vietnamese population. The first historic kingdom dates back to 250 B.C. It was founded by An-Duong-Vuong, the sove-

This painted terra-cotta vase, of the Ban Chieng type, dates back to the Bronze Age.

Shown is a bronze lamp-holder found in a tomb at Lach-Truong near Dong Son.

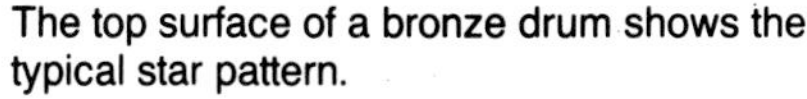

The top surface of a bronze drum shows the typical star pattern.

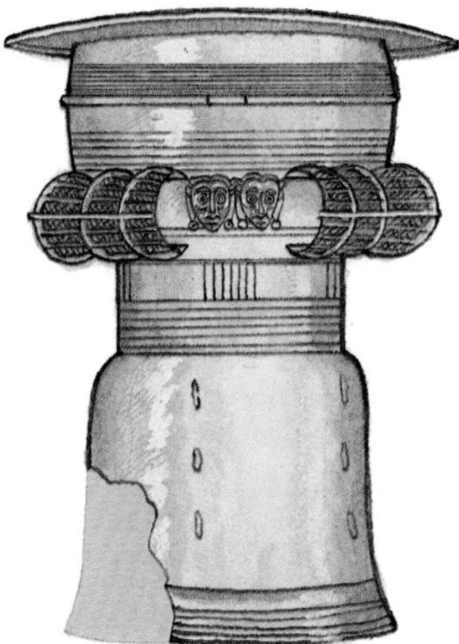

This bronze drum, which was found in Bali, is known as the "moon of Bali."

reign of Au-Lac, and was very open to Chinese influences. Chinese pressure gradually increased until 111 B.C. when the Han general Lou-Po-To wiped out all traces of Vietnamese authority and violently introduced Chinese culture to Vietnam. Within a few years, the Dong Son civilization disappeared completely.

The Persistence of the Stone Civilization

Although the bronze technique took hold along the coastal plains, the use of stone continued on the Indochinese plateau and as far as the island of Sumatra. In these places, its main expressions were in the form of monuments of different sizes. These monuments have been found in various sites and were often associated with burials.

Above is the boat of the dead, as it appears on the bronze drum of Ngoc Lu.

Religion and Cults

Existing drums and tombs give scholars some knowledge of important aspects of the Indochinese and Indonesian populations. The drums were played during rituals for hunting expeditions or for the fertility of the land. For example, they were played to ask for rain. The decorations on the drums were very important. They show shamans, the sun, water, and other symbols of rural life. The people's belief in life after death was often seen in drum decorations. The decorations show boats carrying well-dressed figures. These are the souls of the dead traveling toward the realm of the blessed, which was a great ocean to the east. The drums were also used in burial rituals, when the shaman would use his skills to descend into the realm of the dead and accompany the soul to its destination.

Tombs, another important source of information, were equipped with many objects of daily use. This allowed the dead to supposedly maintain their normal lives. The more architecturally complex tombs, built around the end of the period, were composed of three chambers. The central chamber contained the coffin. The other two contained offerings and bronze lamps with burning flames, the symbol of life.

The boat with the souls of the dead is seen on a cloth from Kroe, on the island of Sumatra.

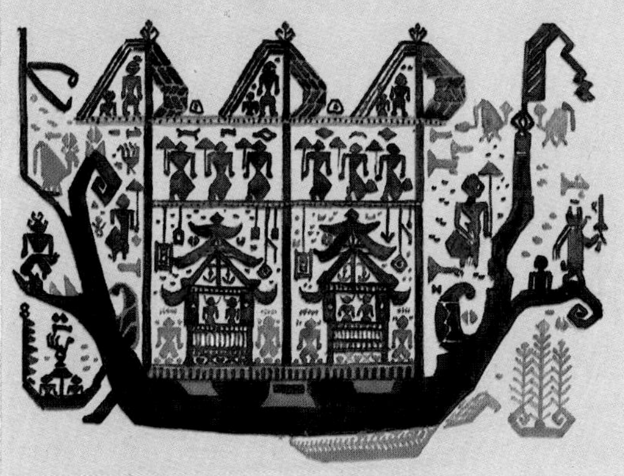

THE BIRTH OF INDOCHINA

Around the first centuries of the Christian Era, the two great political and cultural centers of Asia—China and India—exerted their influence on the Indochinese peninsula. The ideas these cultures brought to the region forever changed its features. First, writing was introduced. Then the great religions of Buddhism and Hinduism spread widely, and finally, complex artistic expression developed.

The Influence of China

When China conquered Vietnam, the country was given Chinese structures, both in its political and administrative organization and in its language and writing. (Chinese became the official language, as well as the first written language of the Vietnamese populations.) Even economic life changed. The whole system of Vietnamese villages was modified according to Chinese models, with permanent rice fields and the regulation of waters.

The Indian Influence

The expansion of India was prompted by trade. During the first century A.D., the Indian people discovered how to take advantage of the prevailing winds that periodically blew toward the land or toward the sea. Thus they began to sail along Asia's southeastern coasts up to the Sunda Islands. There they collected precious and useful goods for trade. They soon established stopover sites along the route where they could store their goods and replenish their food supplies. Eventually they started producing food at these sites. With the Indian people came their writing and their alphabet. Sanskrit, the Indian language, spread as a learned language and was widely spoken. The sacred texts of Hinduism and Buddhism were also widely accepted, as well as mathematical and astronomical concepts which were much more evolved than those of the local populations. Finally, even the Indian political system, built around the figure of the king, was adopted.

The States Influenced by India

During five centuries of Indian influence, numerous states came into being. They were all economically sound and lively cultural centers. The first and most important state was that of Funan. Its influence extended from today's southern Cambodia to the coast of Indonesia, to the Gulf of Siam and to southern Burma. The empire, which ended three centuries later, was ruled by Indian Brahmans and their offspring. The prevailing religion was Brahmanism, but Buddhism was also important. The Indians brought their farming and hydraulic knowledge and created rice fields and channels. The wealth of Funan was contained in its towns, many of which were located inland and connected by a network of channels.

Among the other states which arose at the same time as Funan was the state of Champa. Located on the southern border of the Chinese colonies of the Tonchino region, Champa fought against these colonies in the third and fourth centuries A.D. Its territory, covered by forests of spice trees, gave this state great commercial importance.

The state of Chenla, located along the middle course of the Mekong River, was originally only a small princedom within the state of Funan. At the end of the sixth century A.D., the people of Chenla, the Khmer, conquered Funan and took control of the empire. The Funan civilization, open to sea traveling, was thus replaced by the closed civilization of the Khmer. Their capital was the first great architectural achievement in Cambodia, and the monuments erected there are among the oldest of Indochina.

Populating Oceania

During the first millennium A.D., the process of populating the islands of the Pacific Ocean was completed. The groups of islands scattered in the vast expanses of the ocean are usually divided into: Melanesia, comprising the western-most islands toward New Guinea; Micronesia, including the islands north of New Guinea; and Polynesia, which includes the many islands scattered to the east.

populating Oceania

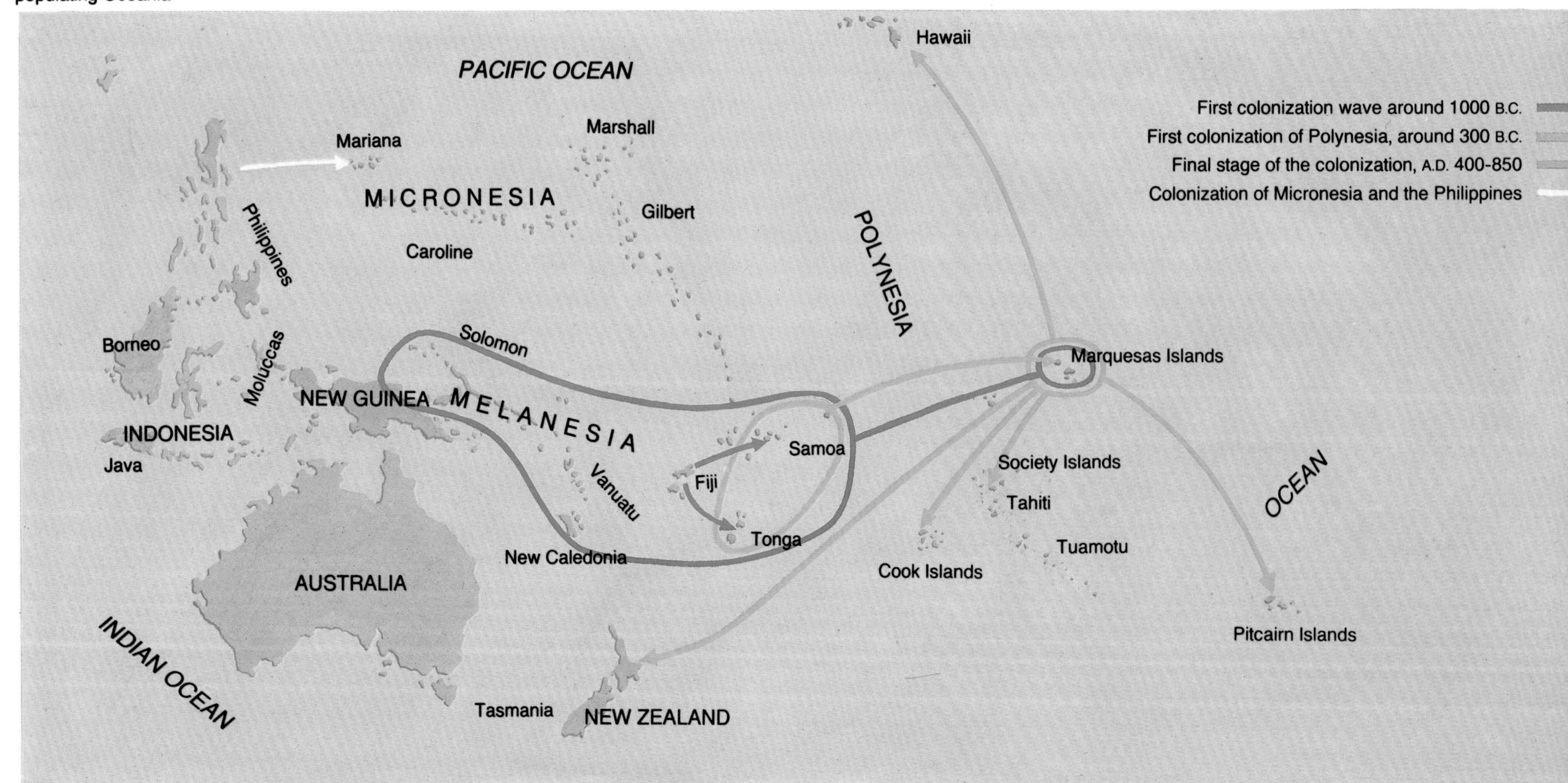

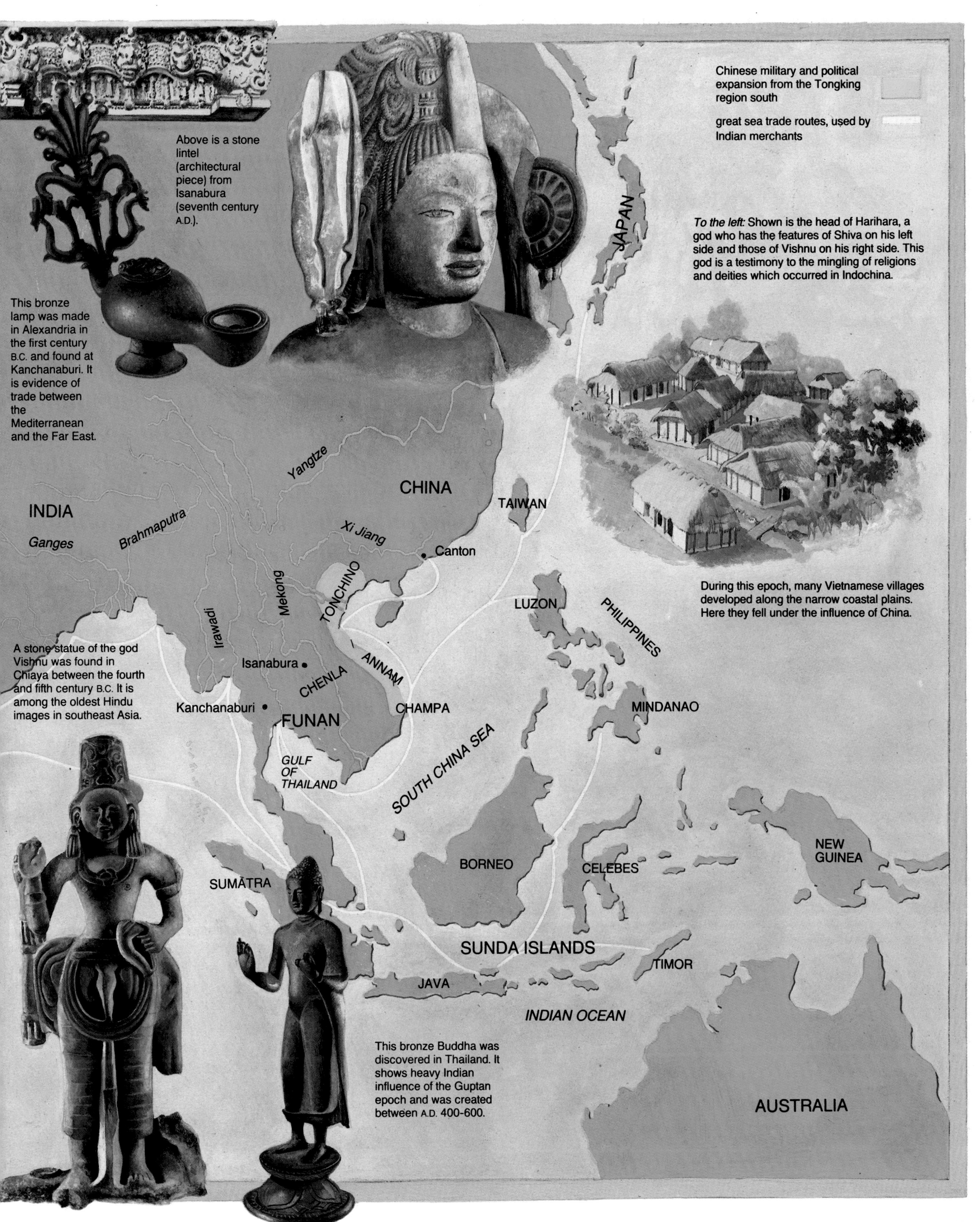

Above is a stone lintel (architectural piece) from Isanabura (seventh century A.D.).

This bronze lamp was made in Alexandria in the first century B.C. and found at Kanchanaburi. It is evidence of trade between the Mediterranean and the Far East.

To the left: Shown is the head of Harihara, a god who has the features of Shiva on his left side and those of Vishnu on his right side. This god is a testimony to the mingling of religions and deities which occurred in Indochina.

During this epoch, many Vietnamese villages developed along the narrow coastal plains. Here they fell under the influence of China.

A stone statue of the god Vishnu was found in Chiaya between the fourth and fifth century B.C. It is among the oldest Hindu images in southeast Asia.

This bronze Buddha was discovered in Thailand. It shows heavy Indian influence of the Guptan epoch and was created between A.D. 400-600.

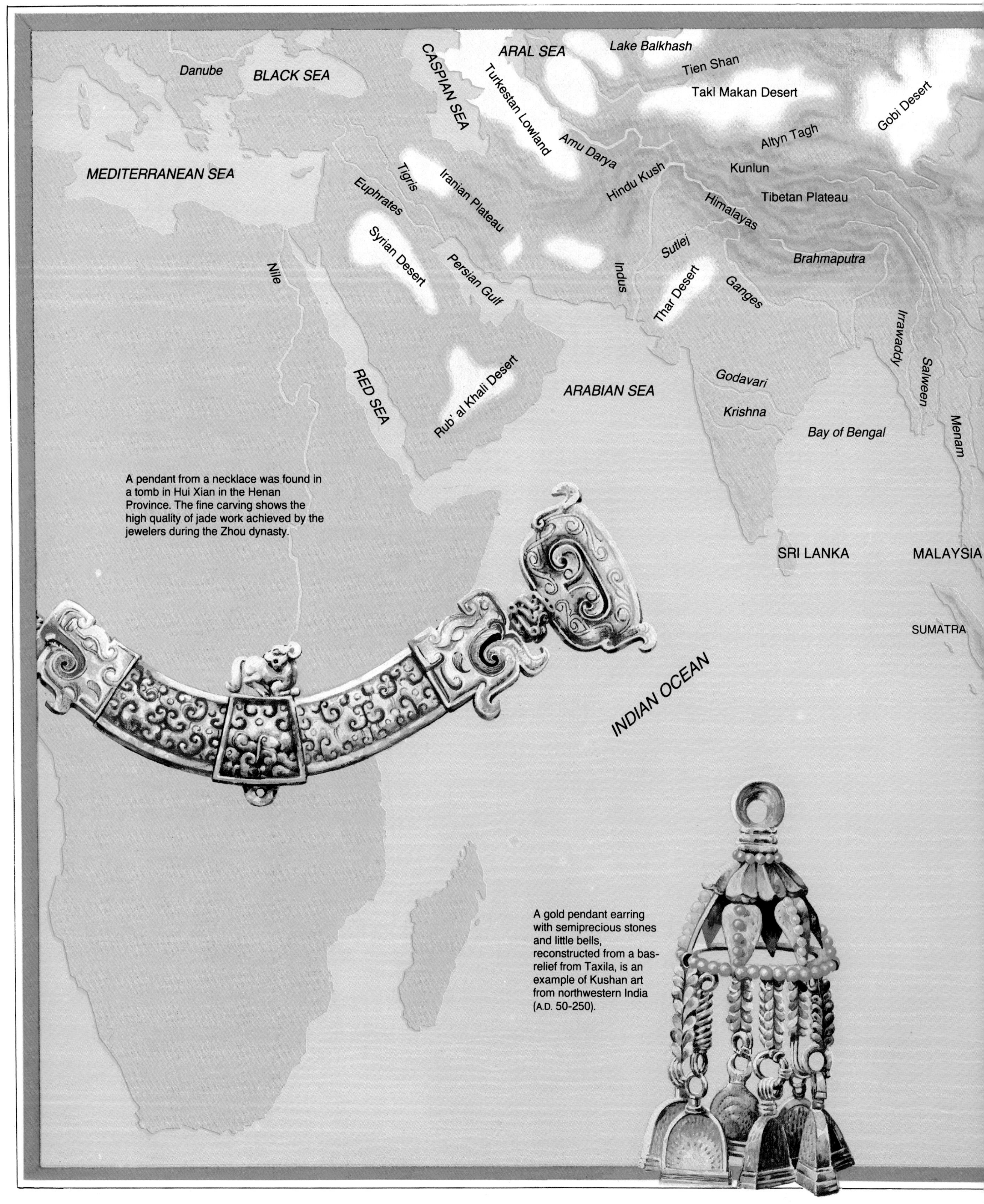

A pendant from a necklace was found in a tomb in Hui Xian in the Henan Province. The fine carving shows the high quality of jade work achieved by the jewelers during the Zhou dynasty.

A gold pendant earring with semiprecious stones and little bells, reconstructed from a bas-relief from Taxila, is an example of Kushan art from northwestern India (A.D. 50-250).

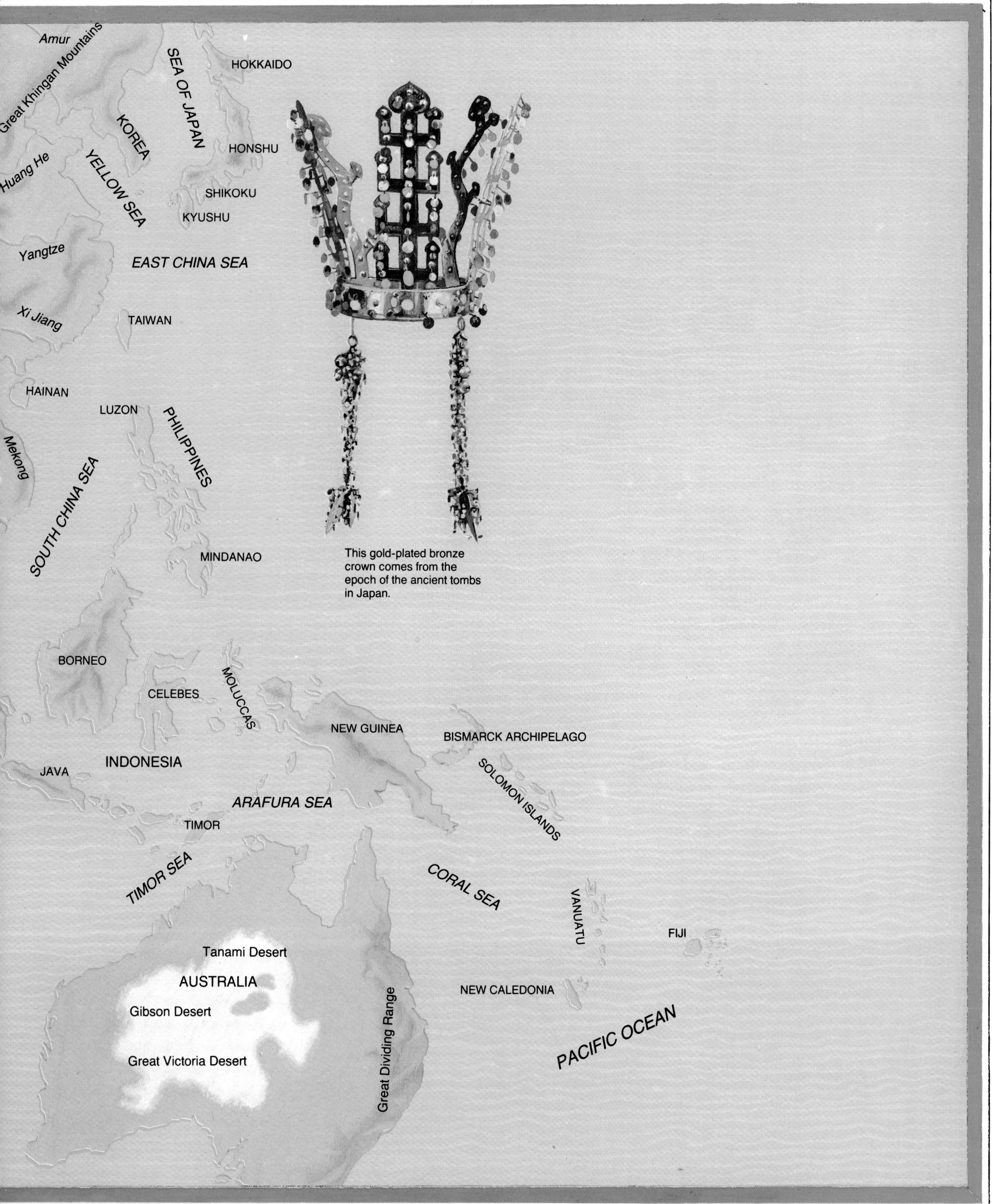

This gold-plated bronze crown comes from the epoch of the ancient tombs in Japan.

GLOSSARY

abundant: very plentiful; more than sufficient.

agriculture: the science and activities of farming; the work of cultivating the earth, producing crops, and raising animals.

archaeology: the scientific study of the life and culture of ancient peoples. Archaeology involves the digging up and uncovering of ancient cities, with all their relics and remains.

artifacts: objects made by people, especially simple or primitive tools, containers, and weapons.

ascetic: a person who leads a life of quiet study and rigid self-denial for religious purposes.

basin: all the land that is drained by a river and its branches. Water collects near a basin to form lakes.

caste: separate social classes based on birth and wealth. The caste system was a typical feature of the Vedic culture of India.

cavalry: fighting troops mounted on horses.

ceramics: the art of making objects of baked clay, such as pottery and earthenware. Ceramics were perfected in India and Southeast Asia between 2500 and 1000 B.C.

continent: one of the principal land masses of the earth. Africa, Antarctica, Asia, Europe, North America, South America, and Australia are regarded as continents.

crossbow: an ancient weapon consisting of a bow set perpendicular to a wooden stock. The stock directs an arrow and is notched to hold a bowstring, which is released by a trigger.

cult: a systematic ritual of religious worship.

culture: the customs, art, and philosophies of a given people at a certain time in history; civilization.

currency: the medium of exchange, or money used, in any country or region.

decade: a period of ten years.

deity: the state of being a god; having a divine nature.

destiny: fate; that which will certainly happen to any person or thing.

divination: the process of attempting to foretell the future or the unknown by magical, mystical, or religious means.

domesticate: to tame wild animals and breed them for a variety of purposes. Hogs and cows are examples of domesticated animals.

dominion: rule or power to rule; supreme authority; a territory or country which is governed by a ruler.

dynasty: a series of rulers who are all from the same family; the period of time during which a specific family rules.

ecology: the relationship between organisms and their environment. The science of ecology is extremely important as a means of preserving all the forms of life on earth.

environment: the circumstances or conditions of a plant or animal's surroundings. The physical and social conditions of an organism's environment influence its growth and development.

epic: a long narrative poem in a formal style about the brave actions and adventures of a traditional or historical hero or heroes.

epigraph: an inscription on a building or monument; a motto or quotation placed at the beginning of a book or chapter.

epoch: the beginning of a new and important period in history; a period of time considered in terms of important events, developments, or persons.

equator: an imaginary circle around the earth, equally distant at all points from both the North Pole and the South Pole. The equator divides the earth's surface into the Northern Hemisphere and the Southern Hemisphere.

evolution: a gradual process in which something changes into a different and usually more complex or better form. Groups of organisms may change with the passage of time so that descendants differ physically from their ancestors.

excavate: to make a hole or cavity by digging; to form by hollowing out; to uncover by digging.

fossil: a remnant or trace of an organism of a past geologic age, such as a skeleton or leaf imprint, embedded in some part of the earth's crust. Scientists search for fossils as a way of learning about past life.

graphics: the art of making drawings according to mathematical rules and principles.

harpoon: a spearlike weapon used in hunting whales and large fish. The early Japanese perfected a harpoon with a mobile point for their fishing needs.

humid: containing a large amount of water or water vapor; damp. Warm air currents floating through coastal areas produce a humid climate.

hydraulic: operated by the motion and force of a liquid.

inscription: something engraved. Many Japanese swords from the third to fourth centuries have inscriptions of ancient writings.

kiln: a furnace or oven for drying or baking something, such as ceramics, bread, or bricks.

lacquer: a stocky varnish obtained from certain trees in China and Japan used to a give a hard, polished finish to wood.

lava: melted rock which flows from an erupting volcano.

legend: a story handed down for generations among a people and believed to be based on actual happenings.

loess: a very fine and fertile soil found mainly in North America, Asia, and Europe. Loess is deposited primarily by the wind.

melancholy: the condition of being sad, gloomy, or depressed.

mercenary: hired soldiers; soldiers paid to fight battles in foreign countries.

migrate: to move from place to place in search of food and shelter. Migration usually revolves around seasonal changes.

minority: a small portion of an otherwise large group; less than half of the whole.

mint: to make money or other currency which is authorized by the government.

moat: a deep, broad ditch dug around a fortress or castle. A moat is often filled with water as a protection against invaders.

monarch: the primary ruler of a state or kingdom, such as a king or queen.

monologue: a long speech delivered by one person. Ancient Greek actors often delivered monologues.

monsoon: a seasonal wind of the Indian Ocean and Asia, blowing from the southwest from April to October, and from the northeast during the rest of the year.

nomad: a member of a tribe or people having no permanent home, but roaming about constantly in search of food and shelter.

oligarchy: a government run by a few select people.

oracle: any person who is believed to be capable of communication with the gods.

orator: a person who is skilled at delivering speeches in public.

patrician: in the society of ancient Rome, a member of a noble or prominent family. Most political positions of that time were held by patricians.

peninsula: a land area almost entirely surrounded by water and connected to the mainland by a narrow strip of earth called an isthmus.

pessimism: the attitude toward life that the worst will always happen; the belief that more bad than good exists in the world.

plateau: a high, level stretch of land.

plebeian: in the society of ancient Rome, one of the common people or the lower classes.

polis: a city-state in ancient Greece. Involvement in the business of the polis meant involvement in politics.

polytheism: the belief in or worship of many gods or more than one god.

prehistoric: referring to a period of time before recorded history.

primitive: of or existing in the beginning or the earliest times; ancient.

produce: fresh fruit and vegetables.

prologue: an introduction; the first part or portion of a literary work used as preparation for what follows.

retreat: to move away from a place of danger toward a place of safety.

revenue: income; the money which a business or government is able to generate for itself through taxation, profit, and other sources.

ritual: a system of acts or procedures, especially with regard to religious worship.

sanctuary: a place of peace or safety; a haven or place of rest; a special building set aside for holy worship.

Sanskrit: an ancient literary language in India begun in the fourth century B.C. Sanskrit is still used today by the followers of the Buddhist religion.

savanna: a grassy plain having only a few trees, especially in tropical or subtropical regions.

shaman: a Buddhist monk; a priest or medicine man who is capable of communicating with good and evil spirits.

steppe: any of the great plains of Southeast Europe and Asia, having few trees.

temperate: a climate which is neither very cold nor very hot, but rather moderate.

terrace: a raised, flat mound of earth with sloping sides.

INDEX

I, J

K

L

M

N, O

P, Q

R